HEIÐA

HEIÐA

A SHEPHERD AT THE
EDGE OF THE WORLD

Steinunn Sigurðardóttir

Translated by Philip Roughton

JOHN MURRAY

First published in Iceland in 2016 by Bjartur
First published in Great Britain in 2019 by John Murray (Publishers)
An Hachette UK company

1

Copyright © Steinunn Sigurðardóttir and Heiða Gudny Ásgeirsdóttir 2016
Translation © Philip Roughton 2019

A CIP catalogue record for this title is available from the British Library

Hardback ISBN 978-1-473-69650-1
Trade Paperback ISBN 978-1-473-69647-1
eBook ISBN 978-1-473-69649-5

Typeset in Simoncini Garamond by Hewer Text UK Ltd, Edinburgh
Printed and bound by CPI Group (UK) Ltd, Croydon, CR0 4YY

John Murray policy is to use papers that are natural, renewable
and recyclable products and made from wood grown in sustainable
forests. The logging and manufacturing processes are expected to
conform to the environmental regulations of the country of origin.

John Murray (Publishers)
Carmelite House
50 Victoria Embankment
London EC4Y 0DZ

www.johnmurray.co.uk

CONTENTS

INTRODUCTION

A friend came to me in the spring of 2015 while I was working on a novel in my hut in south-east Iceland and said categorically: 'You must meet Heiða!' My friend explained that Heiða was a hero, struggling to protect her farmland against being bought by a private energy company. And that this reserved person had been forced into public life, into local politics, even founding an environmental party, to keep up the fight.

Thoroughly intrigued, I set off to visit Heiða at her farm, less than an hour's drive from my hut.

Even from some distance away, she looked like an apparition climbing out of the high seat of her tractor, 181 centimetres tall, slim, with long blond hair. A mixture of an elongated elf and a valkyrie. Then, Heiða having greeted me with the same courteous reserve I recognized from the childhood summers spent at my uncle and aunt's farm in this district, we sat down together at her kitchen table and talked, and talked.

I was so enthralled by her story that I had decided within 10 minutes that this would be my next book. Although my plan was fixed, I did not talk about it to Heiða until I phoned her a week later. I was somewhat taken aback when she instantly agreed because I had seen her deep reserve and understood how much it was against her nature to talk about herself. She explained that her motivation for going ahead was that she needed the story of her lonely struggle to be heard.

This was my motivation too. In the week that had passed between Heiða's kitchen table and our telephone conversation, I had thought long and hard how best to construct this book. After all, it takes more than a fascinating subject for a novelist to turn herself into a non-fiction writer overnight.

I might not have had the courage, were it not for Svetlana Alexievich's wonderful oral histories. People needed to hear this woman's voice too. One of the hardest challenges was preserving Heiða's unique style of speech (a mixture of modern and old-fashioned) and making it look right on the page. Luckily I had started my writing career as a journalist for a daily newspaper in Reykjavik and the experience of conducting innumerable interviews for newspapers, radio and television – since the age of seventeen – stood me in good stead. The research and the writing took place as conversations between us, but in the end, I determined that I needed to make the author, myself, invisible, in order to make the reader feel they are listening to Heiða speak. I struggled at first to find the right shape for the book, but once I landed on the idea of using the seasons as chapters, it all clicked.

It wasn't just that I had to lay aside my novel and become invisible in my new book, I also had to sacrifice my routine. I am a lark rather than an owl but often the only time she was free to talk was late in the evening. Heiða's workload was such that I had to fit in or abandon the project and this book was worth a year of late nights.

Heiða and I were both very nervous about how the book would be received. It felt like a huge responsibility to bring a real person to life, especially when there were still local animosities about the Búland power plant. What a humiliation it would have been to her, how wonderful for her enemies, had the book not worked out.

But it did. Heiða became famous overnight, and as for myself, my readers and critics were equally amazed at this fiction-writer's chameleon act inside a true story. Our book went on to become Iceland's third bestselling title in 2016 and it won two awards. What particularly struck me about its reception was how it spoke to all sorts of people. Young women – from university students to farmers – saw Heiða as their inspiration, taking her destiny into her own hands. Men saw Heiða as their accomplished daughter and felt proud of her. Farmers loved to see their lives depicted. City people loved to learn about life at a remote farm. Now I am hoping that it will show people throughout the world outside our country what our Icelandic temperament and way of life is like . . .

Heiða's life will never be the same again. In Iceland she is now active not only in local politics. She has now given her first speech in Parliament, as a stand-in for the Green Party representative in her south-east constituency. She insists, however, that the main benefit of the book for her was giving other people in her situation the courage to stand up and protest.

While it is undeniable that her temper is every bit as volcanic as our lava-filled land, we became fast friends during the making of this book, and remain so to this day. And my interest in Heiða, her work, her life and times, remains as keen today as it was on the day I made my decision at the kitchen table in Ljótarstaðir, her farm.

Steinunn Siguðardóttir, February 2019

My farm, Ljótarstaðir, has been occupied continuously since the twelfth century, as evidenced by the tephra layers revealed in excavations.

There are various theories about my farm's name. One is that it's after the original settler Ljótur, who's supposedly buried in a mound here. Another is that it's a variant of the female name Ljótunn. But the loveliest theory, and the one that I'm going to stick with, I heard by chance recently at a district museum in the north. A staff member there connected the farm name Ljótarstaðir with an old expression that I hadn't heard before, which has to do with light. The expression is *Birtunni ljótar yfir*: the light brightens, shines over; that is, as if drawing slowly over the land, as at dawn.

This makes sense, as the terrain surrounding Ljótarstaðir is open and the sun comes up early here. At Snæbýli, the other farm in the valley, the sun appears later, at the foot of the mountain to the north.

So, Ljótarstaðir means 'The farm where the light is'. That's my farm.

*   *   *

On the way home, I always like coming by Fitarholt Hill. I sometimes stop there to look over at Ljótarstaðir and my royal blue rooftops, across the valley called Krókur. From Fitarholt you can see far into the interior, to the mountains beyond the Tungufljót River. The view extends to Mýrdalsjökull Glacier, behind the mountains west and north of Ljótarstaðir – the tallest being Kvalningshnúkar and Fjalldalsbrún. Also visible are the highland pastures in Skaftártunga and Álftaver.

The buildings at Ljótarstaðir stand at an elevation of almost two hundred metres, and the terrain rises sharply behind them. So my land, which is vast by Icelandic standards, is mainly wilderness beyond the boundary of the highlands.

Our local place names testify to how extreme winter can be here: Snjóagil (Snow Ravine) at Ljótarstaðir and Snjódalagljúfur (Snow Valley Gorge) at Snæbýli (Snow Farm); and the grass only turns green late in the spring. So living and farming in this rugged area is hardly sought-after, let alone all on your own. I recently read a blog describing my farm as being on the 'border of the inhabitable world'. It was far from the first time I've heard this kind of remark – and usually it's followed by the comment that the only things that could survive here are foxes and ravens.

So it's ironic, really, that I've had to fight so hard from the very start for the right to be here. The last and by far the toughest battle began in 2010, and was what pushed me into local politics. The planned construc-tion of the Búland Power Plant would extend over the entire Skaftártunga area, from the Hólaskjól Highland

Centre in the north to the Ring Road in the south, with a stop at Ljótarstaðir: a sixty-metre-high dam in my gorge. It would be as high as the tower of Hallgrímskirkja Cathedral in Reykjavik. A ten-square-kilometre reservoir would be located approximately four kilometres as the crow flies from my laundry room door. And on my best pastureland too, where the grass grows first in the spring.

It's not exactly high on the wish list of a solitary farmer with five hundred sheep to take on the time-consuming and virtually unpaid responsibility of a position on the municipal council. But I have to defend the countryside, my own land and our very way of life. This has cost me an almost inhuman amount of effort.

SUMMER

SUMMER

I'm husbandless, yes – but that's me to blame.
To tell you the truth, I don't think it a shame.
My mum does the chores
that need doing indoors,
while I potter outside. Farming's my game.

TRACTOR

Summer is a fantastic season, full of greenery, growth and light. But I have no time to spare for rolling naked in the dewy grass in the evening, which according to the old folk tale can heal you of all sorts of ailments, particularly at midsummer. Night-time is for sleeping, and by the end of my long working day I'm far too tired to indulge in any other behaviour. And, as it happens, in the summer I actually spend most of my time inside – in the cab of my tractor, that is.

It's home to me. I pretty much grew up on a tractor. It was a brake-less Massey Ferguson. Naturally, it was cab-less as well, meaning I spent my time out under the open sky ... where the sunlight poured straight into my veins and left me completely, radiantly suntanned. But there's no chance of that in my current tractor cab.

I really like driving tractors. They're useful for far more than just raking and mowing. One of my favourite activities is coming up with verses while at the wheel. My whole family loves poetry. My sister Arndís, who died when she was seventeen, was an enthusiastic, clever poet. My sisters, Ásta, Fanney and I frequently attend poetry meet-ups, or what we might call, for fun, 'rhymesters' conventions'. And we really enjoy trading verses with each other.

Mum and Dad taught us girls all kinds of verses and poems by rote. And wonderful rhythms and images became fixed in our memories – as in the following:

Instinct now inflames each steed.
Hoofbeats hammer hard the field.
Fell and dale fall silent, heed
manes that whip with force they wield.
As each racer unleashed flies,
lips drip foam and nostrils flare.
Sweat streams from the croup and thighs.
Frenzied neighs cut through the air.

(*Steeds*, Einar Benediktsson)

Bjarni from Vogur was our great-grandfather on our mother's side. That's where we get our poet's blood. It helps that there are also good poets on my father's side of the family, and that Dad was particularly sharp-witted and sarcastic. Plus Mum is a bookworm, with a deep love of the Icelandic language. She also used to write her own verses, but says that when my sisters and I started really getting into it, she decided to give up.

I've always enjoyed arranging words, making verses click. I started as a kid, and even then I could hear whether a poem was composed well or poorly. You either have the knack or you don't.

And when I'm in the tractor, I do more than write poetry. I love dancing so I dance there, too. But for that I could definitely do with the cab being a bit bigger. My neighbour loaned me his big tractor once and it was perfect for dancing in – the height of luxury.

My tractor cab can also be my office as I end up doing a lot of business from it whenever possible. I spend a great deal of time on my phone, sending emails, while I'm raking, tedding and mowing, but only in my fields, of course, not out on the road.

I've also figured out how to post on Snapchat while driving the tractor with one hand. I eat lots of fruit in the cab, too. I just toss the banana skins, orange peel and apple cores out the window as I go. Decorations for the hay.

I drive a Valtra A 95, 2007 model. This, my good old Grey, is an economic-boom tractor, as the model year indicates. It's one of the many found on Icelandic farms. It's my main tractor, used for everything except tedding the hay. For that, I use my Massey Ferguson 165, 1974 model. It goes by the name of Grímur, and is the last remaining tractor from when I was a kid. The others were all sold – the last to pay for the complete overhaul of Grímur, which was in pretty bad shape.

I take good care of my old Grey. It's usually clean and polished and in decent shape, but it's nine years old and has done a lot of miles. It's vital that I keep it well maintained because it can be my workplace for hours and sometimes days at a time. Grímur is what's called a Harlem tractor: a cheap and simple variety, bouncy and lacking in luxury but at the same time robust, reliable and low-maintenance. It gets the job done, and that's fine, but I have to admit that I really wouldn't mind having a better, more comfortable tractor, such as a new and bigger Valtra or any other dependable, low-maintenance model with a hydraulic reverser. A shiftless transmission would be tops, along with a sprung front axle and an air seat, just the thing for a very-soon-to-be middle-aged woman. An audio system with a USB port, along with slightly more room for my darling Fífill (Dandelion), would be a real bonus.

According to the hour meter in my Grey, it has run for an average of 517 hours a year for the past nine years. That's approximately 21 days and nights or 42 twelve-hour working days. Of course, my usage varies greatly depending on the season . . . but as I said before, my summers are spent mainly in the tractor.

The amount of work with farm machinery done by women in Iceland seems to vary from district to district, but here in Skaftártunga it's always been common for girls to drive tractors. In this area, there's generally no distinction between men's work and women's work.

Long shifts in the tractor take a definite physical toll. I can put up with twelve-hour working days in the tractor, but any longer and I really start to feel it. There's so much effort involved in getting the hay all cut, baled and gathered that I don't leave the tractor unnecessarily – I pause only to fill its tank or stop and eat. I don't even go back to the house for meals. Mum drives the Lux out to the hayfields to bring me food. For haymaking, I work together with my neighbour Palli from Hvammur because, like me, he farms on his own. When we're cutting his grass, his mum and dad do the cooking and bring us meals – if his wife is at work, that is.

Hours spent sitting in an inflexible tractor are, of course, not good for the back. One good counter-stretch I've learned is to hang off the loader, like laundry on the line.

It can also get uncomfortably hot in the cab when the sun is shining. Mine isn't air-conditioned and I can't normally have the windows open because it's so loud, especially when pulling heavy machinery and at high rpms. More expensive tractors have better engine compartments, whereas old ones like mine make quite a racket. I do love its engine though, despite its loudness. It's dependable and powerful: frankly I'm happy as long as it starts and does its job.

Fífill has accompanied me in the cab since he was tiny. Now he's so big that he takes up practically all the floor. But early on he learned the right way to position himself so that things keep running smoothly. Things did go a bit south the other day, when he was so tired that he turned round and ended up lying heavily on my throttle foot. He weighs so much now that I had to power-lift him with my leg. But he's no danger to my driving – the tractor is slow and has a long response time, and I have decades of experience driving it.

I let Fífill out of the cab now and then, and he runs alongside and has a look around. He hops out himself and I'm sure he could get back in on his own, but I like to make things easier for him. So he puts his front paws up on the step and I lift him in. He has just enough room to turn round. Then I get back in and sit down and he crawls under my legs towards the door, and lies there with his tail on the throttle.

He's already well on his way to his eventual forty kilograms. I feed him twice a day; a half-kilo of offal each time, twice what my old dog eats. But he'll start eating less once he's full-grown. My friend Adda at Herjólfsstaðir tells me that German Shepherds keep growing until they're two.

There's a long history of breeding behind this handsome dog. The woman I got him from, who runs Gunnarsholt Breeding, has been breeding Shepherds for twenty years.

Fífill is a really special creature: gentle and fun, and a wonderful companion. He has recovered fully from his lack of appetite in the spring. I'm out working most of the time during lambing, and he took being left behind badly, didn't sleep enough and then overexerted himself, dropping quite a few kilos as a result. Now he's back at his ideal weight and is my beautiful dog once more. Fífill doesn't get in my way when I dance in the tractor, and in any case, I can dance just with my hands. And he doesn't seem to mind when I sing at the top of my lungs. I love singing and it's great to sing in the tractor.

There was a lot of music when I was little. We sang and sang and sang, at home and in the car. Dad had a beautiful tenor voice. He had a wide range too – both high up and far deep down. If he'd become a singer, he could have gone a long way. He was also a master at reciting ballads, and much sought-after at gatherings here. And Mum is a very fine soprano. She was always in the church choir, and still is. Sadly, none of us sisters has inherited her beautiful singing voice, but that hasn't stopped us.

I listen to music all the time, all kinds of music, including male choirs. Pretty much anything, really, from AmabAdamA to Páll Óskar. Not to mention the old heavy metal dudes in Guns N' Roses, Metallica and AC/DC – they're the best.

Mum knows a great many song lyrics, from musicals, revues and whatnot. My sisters and nieces and I have all ended up with what my Aunt Birna calls 'jukebox syndrome'. If we hear a name, we immediately start singing a song connected with it. Even rhythmical sounds such as hammering or hoof-beats can get me singing. But my favourite tunes of all to sing are Christmas songs. For some reason, even though it's completely the wrong time of year, I'm always singing them during lambing!

My head is packed full of lyrics, show tunes and poems. On the other hand, I can never remember what number oil filter the tractor has.

HEIÐA AT A PUBLIC MEETING

I find this world beautiful wherever I go, and don't hesitate to express it. Every place has its charms, but my mountain landscape is particularly dear to me. Yet when I was a kid, farmers didn't get teary-eyed over crags, escarpments or dewdrops in the grass, or at least they were more careful to hide their tears. Sometimes when people visited us in the old days, their eyes practically popped out at the views of the surrounding mountains and the blueness of the Tungufljót River. But when they kept going on about how beautiful it all was, my old dad got embarrassed and changed the subject, herding them all inside for coffee, just to put a stop to their sentimental drivel.

ÁSGEIR AND THE GIRLS

My parents, sisters and I always did all the farm work together. My father Ásgeir was really good at sharing out chores and always took us along with him. He pulled us on a toboggan out to the sheep shed when we were little – until we were able to totter there ourselves. We were called 'Ásgeir and the girls', and it wasn't just here at home that we put our collective noses to the grindstone . . . we also all helped out in various communal projects in this area.

My big sisters were total Vikings. When Ásta was a teenager, Dad started taking her along with him on the round-ups in the highland pastures. These days there's always a bunch of women on the round-ups, though my friend Ella and I have been going the longest. Soon it'll be almost a quarter of a century since we first went – it was on horseback then, whereas nowadays both of us ride quad bikes.

We just take it for granted here in Skaftártunga that women do as much farm work as men. As a matter of fact, Ella's sister Oddný Steina and I thought it was a joke when we first heard someone talking about 'men's work' at the farmers' college (now the agricultural university) in Hvanneyri. But we were the only ones who laughed.

It went on like that all winter. Attending the college with us were all kinds of bold, intelligent farm girls who'd never driven a tractor, never changed an oil filter, never shovelled dung to any real extent. And we heard it again and again. Men's work! Women's work! Oddný Steina and I were gobsmacked. She'd been raised just like me, even though she grew up with two brothers, whereas in my house there were only girls (though sometimes a boy or two in the summers). But Oddný Steina and I have both nailed corrugated iron sheets onto roofs hundreds of times ... changed tyres, on tractors too, of course, and done all the other jobs that men do. It was no big deal, and no one else we knew found it remarkable.

The only reason that I'm able to do all that I can is because I've never been undervalued, never been told that I couldn't do this or that because I was a woman. During my early years of farming, no neighbour ever hesitated to ask me to come help pour concrete or whatever other job they had to do. And I always lend a hand in community projects with my tools and equipment.

I enjoy all types of work, if it goes well. Especially construction. I think it's great when a big project comes up. If it's a major undertaking or a real challenge, then I'm in my element. But I'm a total loser when it comes to cooking.

When I was little, I was told that I could start farming as soon as I'd got a husband. But I never understood that: why should I need a husband to run a farm? Obviously, I still don't get it, after all these years. Furthermore, I really don't like the common expression 'farmer's wife', and never use it. It implies that a woman can't be a farmer in her own right, just a wife. Just so it's clear, I'm Heiða the farmer, like any other woman who runs a farm.

Ella from Úthlíð, which is a farm here in Skaftártunga not far from Ljótarstaðir, and I are both unmarried, childless and run our own farms. We're childhood friends and began farming around the same time, at the age of twenty-three. Not having children was a conscious decision on my part. Whether it's the same for her, or whether she's set her heart on having a family eventually, I have no idea. I don't recall it ever having come up, in fact. Ella and I have always had plenty of other things to talk about.

THE UGLY DUCKLING

As a kid, I was small and wimpy. And I was also extremely thin. There was something wrong with my wrist. I had what's called a scaphoid fracture, an injury that's not uncommon in children. I was given injections and had to wear a brace. I also had to avoid sudden hand movements, which could throw it all out of whack again. It was a problem for many years.

Even with my bad wrist, I always had to do my chores. But I felt like such a wimp. I was listless and bad at sports. A weakling. A late developer, physically. And the ugliest creature on earth. With glasses.

I was sent away from home to boarding school in Kirkjubæjarklaustur at the age of eight. Back then, kids didn't take the school bus daily to and from school as they do nowadays; instead, we stayed at the boarding school in Klaustur five days a week. Those were difficult winters for me. Everyone used to bad-mouth the teachers, which only served to make me dislike both them and the rest of the school. It was a weird kind of tradition, back then, for everyone to disparage everything about school.

Of course school was fun sometimes, but in general I was terribly homesick, and often rather depressed. Added to which I was expected to look after myself, as an eight-year-old girl: take showers and wash and comb my hair. I had long hair and made a complete mess of it.

I cried a lot during those boarding-school years, but to be honest I wasn't the only one. There was often a chorus of crying girls at bedtime, wailing and whining away.

We learned to swim in Klaustur, which was useful in and of itself, but I never got over my fear of the water and I didn't like swimming – and still don't.

It wasn't all bad though. I made other good friends at school, besides Ella. For instance, there was Dísa, and Þórdís from Hraungerði in Álftaver, who's now a mathematics professor in Norway. We did so well in our lessons that Dísa and I were moved up a class, which meant that our schooling was one year shorter. Another bonus was when the kids from Hraungerði were driven to school, and I got to go with them for two years, staying at Ásar with my sister Ásta and my brother-in-law Dóri. That immediately made things much more bearable. But overall it still felt as if we spent far too many winters stuck at boarding school.

It did give me time to read every single book in the library at Klaustur, though. Now I don't have that kind of time to spare, but I still enjoy reading and do so quickly. Halldór Laxness is a favourite of mine; I love his way of thinking and use of language, if not always his approach to a story. But he can say in one sentence what others can't even say in half a page.

I drank in all those books and longed to experience and be a part of it all. I wanted to be the shepherd girl with her flute, grazing her sheep all summer and knowing all the birds and the waterfalls. The prettiest girl at the dance during the herring years – when Iceland's coasts were teeming with that fish and people flocked to work at the fishing villages. The half-frozen sailor clinging to the rigging in a horrendous storm, speaking last words before being swept into the sea, never to be seen again. Tom Swift, who could invent and build everything that he and his friends needed for their adventures. The boy who owned the horse called Gustur. The girl in *White Bread with Jam* by Kristín Steinsdóttir. The English jockey who was injured so badly saving her beloved father that she could never compete again, but who then found joy and fulfilment in training and taking care of the horses that her husband then competed on. Closest to my heart were the books that led me into other worlds, such as the Narnia stories.

It could be a bit complicated getting home from boarding school in Klaustur at weekends, and then back again. Snow ploughing was done differently in those days, and the road home could often be impassable for a large part of the winter. It was often easier to get to Snæbýli because the milk had to be picked up from there no matter what, so the farmers there ploughed the road clear with their tractors. Sometimes the school bus driver would bring me home on a snowmobile. Or Valur, Ella's dad, or Dóri would, too.

Sometimes I had to trudge the final stretch through the snow, from the bridge over the Tungufljót River where the road divided to Snæbýli in the south and Ljótarstaðir in the north. These two heath farms are the only ones in the valley, at the margin of the highlands. Ljótarstaðir is the highest farm 'beyond the river', as it's described; that is, the highest farm in Skaftártunga, west of the Tungufljót River. The road ends at Ljótarstaðir.

We were very isolated up there. As a child, I was so lonely that I invented an imaginary friend, who stayed around right up until my teenage years. Her name was María, and she was quite a boisterous character. Sometimes I would scream loudly if she'd been inadvertently stepped on. Once or twice my sister Fanney got really annoyed with her. Yet Fanney can't have thought that badly of my María seeing as she went on to give her daughter the same name.

At home, great emphasis was laid on avoiding all unnecessary trips and on being frugal. We had no snowmobile or other vehicle that would have made it easier for us to get through the heavy snow.

When I really wanted to learn to play the accordion, that idea fell on deaf ears. Nor did I ever get the toys that I wanted most, such as a Stiga snow-racer. But Fanney more than anyone understood how I felt, and once she started working, she bought me all sorts of fun toys, like a remote-controlled car and a doll from the Quelle catalogue.

In turn I made sure that María, Fanney's daughter, got the things that I never did. I gave her a snow-racer, for instance. And she got to play to her heart's content on my quad bike from the day she was big enough to clamber onto its seat – according to strict rules at first, just driving it in a circle here in the farmyard. She and my nephew Sæmundur played constantly on my quad, and I spent tons on gas for it. We had a huge amount of fun on the snowmobile as well when we first got it. We just drove and drove and it was hard to get us back inside the house.

My friend Linda was here in the countryside with us every summer for ten years, longer than anyone else. Her last summer here was when I was sixteen. She'd been selected for the junior division of the national ski team and had to train hard. So we trained together, running and doing all kinds of strength and conditioning exercises. Linda was a truck: incredibly strong, whereas I was little more than a candlewick in comparison. Starting with that summer, things changed, and I began growing stronger.

Then at sixteen, I got contact lenses. That helped my self-esteem and self-confidence. Both had been low but have improved gradually, to the point where I've learned to trust myself, as the self-help books say – or so I'm told. On the other hand, I've always been shy interacting with others, even if that might not be obvious on the outside. I used to be so shy that I found making small talk at gatherings really uncomfortable. But once I began doing pregnancy scanning of sheep I had to interact with a lot of different people, working with them and having coffee, sharing meals and staying at farms all over the country. It's been an excellent learning experience.

I attended secondary school in Skógar for two years. At the time, I was still such a gangly teenager that none of my clothes ever fitted me. I felt like an ugly scarecrow. On top of that, I was still at the stage at which I blamed myself for anything that went wrong. I couldn't face moving from my small school in Skógar to the big comprehensive school in Selfoss. Instead I went to work, taming horses with Jónas at Norður-Hvammur in Mýrdalur.

Unlike my home, Norður-Hvammur is a farm that's very much on the beaten track; something was always going on there. Swedish girls often worked there, and sometimes other foreigners stayed there, so things felt very different to back home at Ljótarstaðir, where not even a single person might stop by for half the winter when everything was buried deep in snow.

I was so introverted when I first worked at Norður-Hvammur that they could hardly get a word out of me. And I was so embarrassed about my height that I went around with my head and shoulders perpetually stooped. Fortunately, they didn't let me get away with it. They started teasing me right from the start.

Drífa, the farmer's daughter, and I clicked immediately and we're still friends today. She's so funny that she would make a fantastic stand-up comic. She said that I would become hunchbacked and my breasts would start to grow inwards if I kept on stooping the way I did. I said that that would be fine . . . because then I would have four eye sockets. Our senses of humour bounced brilliantly off each other. We got each other going and laughed and laughed and play-fought raucously in the tiny old wooden farmhouse.

Otherwise raucousness wasn't exactly my thing. Years later the folks at Norður-Hvammur told me that I was so quiet that I kept scaring the life out of people by suddenly appearing like an apparition after climbing silently up the creaky old timber stairs to the upper floor.

Drífa's mum, Droplaug, was not really what you'd call an ordinary Icelandic countrywoman: she was a former hippy who'd lived in Copenhagen and enjoyed goofing around with me and Drífa. One day she was playing around doing our make-up in the style of her teenage years, the sixties, with eyeliner and white lips. Then she teased and backcombed our hair and had us try on outfits to match. Droplaug was so amazed at my transformation that she ordered me to call my Aunt Kolla (Kolbrún Aðalsteinsdóttir), who ran the Elite modelling school. When I did, Kolla immediately booked me onto a photo shoot.

Some Italian photographers came, and we did the shoot up on a glacier. I was scared to death of these strangers. The other model was another Icelandic girl who had beautiful wavy red hair and bright green eyes. And there I was, innocent-looking, with blue eyes and pale skin. The photographers were over the moon at the witch and angel in front of them.

After New Year the following winter, I stayed with Kolla and took a course at her modelling school, at the same time as taking a seminar on strengthening my self-esteem. It wasn't all glamour. I also worked processing capelin fish in Keflavík, and for a few days as a temp on a garbage truck in Suðurnes.

In April I took part in a modelling competition in New York and came in second place in the photo-shoot category. I could have tried my luck as a model in New York and Milan, as Kolla had connections. A few big agents got in contact. But I was heading home for lambing, and didn't follow the modelling call. I did a bit of modelling in Iceland afterwards but I wasn't interested in it as a career.

I'd realized that I didn't want to be a model. The modelling I did do was fun, and I don't regret doing it. But even then, I detested the objectification. Modelling felt shallow and pointless. I thought it a very silly idea to earn my living simply by being pretty. And it wasn't fun eating only vegetables and freezing my butt off on a glacier.

I don't like hearing that I'm pretty. I'm kind of tired of it. It makes me think – uh-oh, here we go again! My looks aren't thanks to me; it's just genetics. But pay me compliments about something that I've built . . . and then I melt like chocolate in sunshine!

When I was little, I was never complimented on my appearance, and my sisters and I were taught not to be vain. Nowadays, girls are constantly being told that they're pretty – isn't that taking it a bit too far? Judging by the constant gushing on Facebook, it feels like it is. You put up a photo of yourself in a dress, and then the stream of praise turns on: 'cutie, cutie, cutie'.

Well, no such vain fuss was ever made when I was little. A neighbour cut our hair at home, and I always wore my sisters' hand-me-downs. But when I wanted to have long hair, I was allowed that indulgence. Even now I still don't have the slightest clue about make-up, despite having been a model. All that stuff is like Chinese to me. With me, cosmetics just sit around unused until their expiry date. At most, I know how to put on mascara. But if asked what cosmetics I always keep in my handbag, my answer would have to be lip balm.

On the other hand, I did learn how to walk in high heels while in the business. Apparently quite well, too, because when I put on heels again the other day, something I hadn't done since I was nineteen, I thought that I would fall right on my ass – but nope, flouncing around on those stilts was just like riding a bike.

No one was more surprised by the whole idea of me modelling than I was. But even back then, it was my modus operandi to be up for anything and just go for it. The experience was really exciting, and without a doubt a step forward for me. Kolla remains convinced to this day that I could have become a top model, even though for her the most important thing was helping to strengthen my self-esteem and shake off most of my shyness.

Personally, I never believed that I could earn a living as a model. That career takes a different kind of self-confidence. To show up at a modelling agency alongside a bunch of top-class girls with top-class portfolios, you have to feel confident that you can do exactly what's asked of you every time. Now if it had been a competition to sprint up a slope to catch a sheep, I wouldn't have hesitated. Or if it was to nail down a board. But it just really wasn't my thing to stroll into a modelling agency announcing hey, look at me, here I am, and I'm the prettiest! I didn't like cameras, and still don't. I often lost my nerve on a shoot if, for instance, I was told to dance or to act natural. But if I was told exactly what I should be doing, it was no problem.

Looking back, I wouldn't change a thing: I've never regretted not taking it further. My farming career has lasted so much longer than I would have spent modelling. But to be honest, I hardly ever think back about it . . . I find others are much more interested in this piece of my past than I am. And out here in the countryside, I've always been a bit embarrassed about my modelling stint – doing that instead of digging ditches or engaging in some other proper, useful work.

It certainly can be said that my modelling experience and my stay at Norður-Hvammur was a time of transformation for me. At least it appeared so from the outside, as other people described it as a new person being created. And I have that period of increased self-esteem to thank for pushing myself to enroll that autumn at Selfoss Comprehensive School, earn my diploma and then go to farmers' college in Hvanneyri.

My two years in Hvanneyri were ideal. The courses were fascinating and were attended by young people with the same interests as me. That makes such a big difference. And then there was also the partying and all the fun we had. But otherwise I went home on week-ends to take care of all the farm work that needed doing. Shovelling dung, rounding up sheep, that kind of thing.

The modelling business finally showed me that it was downright desirable to be a beanpole. Growing up I'd got tall so fast that I tried everything I could to make myself shorter. It was so hard to find clothes that fitted: I was lanky and skinny, and shirt sleeves and trouser legs were always too short. That didn't help boost my confidence. Then I started feeling irritated that clothes weren't made for people like me. For the longest time, in fact, I mainly wore the woollen jump-ers that Mum knitted for me, and still does. I just waited for them to come into fashion – which they eventually did.

What irritated me the most was when people said: 'Wow, you're tall!'

The things strangers feel completely free to say are of course absolutely unbelievable. The comments that I got, such as 'You're so skinny! Don't you ever eat anything?'

Even today, people say straight to my face: 'Damn, you're tall!'

It used to upset me but nowadays I don't care any more.

A few years ago, I went to a confirmation party in Akureyri. Afterwards, we went out dancing at a club. All sorts of people were there. A man of around fifty came over and stared at me standing there in my short tight dress and boots. He looked me up and down:

'Man, you're tall! Wow! I don't mean anything negative by it. But you're just really tall!'

He kept going on and on about it until I finally
snapped and said: 'And just you wait till I stand up
straight!'

FARMING BEGINS

Deep down, of course, I was a farmer, and had always wanted to run my own farm. I took over the farming operations at Ljótarstaðir in 2001, after finishing my course at the farmers' college. I was twenty-three at the time.

At the start, things were simple, in that my parents had always kept all their possessions separate . . . everything from framed photographs to the farm machinery and buildings. I only bought Dad's sheep and his farm-support entitlement. I'd already owned a bunch of sheep, and those plus Dad's amounted to almost half the farm's total number.

I also bought smaller equipment and tools from my dad, and we made a kind of operations contract for the tractor, which was the main machine then: it was a newish Case. So you might say that I'd gone into partnership with my mum, because she still owned the buildings and land. But I was free to make whatever changes I wanted regarding all the decisions and responsibilities connected with the farm and the land.

At that time, I was out working a lot, and Dad and Mum took care of the daily chores, such as feeding the sheep. I worked night and day in those first years. I was both teaching in Kirkjubæjarklaustur and renovating the sheep-house at home, which often meant working well into the night. Those first autumns, there was still a Butchers' Association of the South slaughterhouse in Kirkjubæjarklaustur, and I worked there too, along with teaching and everything else. At the slaughter-house, I occasionally did gutting, which is drudgery, but I worked mainly in the freezer, which meant having to show up at five in the morning. It was a great job . . . in -35 degrees Celsius. Women didn't normally work in the freezer, so I had to ask specifically to be allowed to do so. As usual, that wasn't a problem.

When I started farming at Ljótarstaðir much was in disrepair or out-dated; the working methods there had long been old-fashioned in many respects. At least the farm wasn't really the way I wanted it. I was touchy about that and really wanted to make improvements, and that's been my big project for the last fifteen years now. It also irked me that people had been criticizing Ljótarstaðir.

I did all the renovation work myself, albeit with all sorts of assistance. My friend Siggeir, who's a builder, helped me a great deal and also taught me a lot. For instance, I'd never used a circular saw before. I reno-vated the sheep-house entirely in the summer of 2002, and turned its barn into a second sheep-house. This was a major upgrade to our feeding facilities; it was extremely practical and really helped to lighten our workload. Dad had been violently opposed to the changes at first, though he eventually paid them a grudging compliment or two ... admittedly only to others who then reported them back to me.

Dad and I tended to disagree about most things to do with the farm. This led to a lot of arguments once I dared to stand up for myself. I'm a peaceful person by nature and I don't like conflict, so these disagreements took their toll on me. Dad was famous for his acerbity. The words we exchanged weren't always the prettiest – whenever I managed to get a word in, that is, because I tend to freeze up if I get angry. The times that I managed to say my piece, I really tried to be louder than him – but it was difficult because that man had a very strong voice.

At one point before I finally took over, everything came to a head: we had a huge fight and I packed my bags and was out of there. The other day, Jónas and Droplaug were reminiscing about how furious I'd been when I told them what had happened. I apparently concluded my rant with 'This time I've had it with that bastard.' So I left for six months. But then it suddenly struck me that Dad had got away with it! It had been my intention to farm at Ljótarstaðir, so why shouldn't I do so? I went back home and wasn't welcomed very warmly at first . . . but things got better.

I look a lot like my dad. Just think – two people who look almost exactly the same standing eyeball to eyeball and arguing like hell. Both long and thin. The same nose. The same eyes. Their mannerisms and movements similar, and, not least, the way they speak and their retorts.

I composed a verse about this for a poetry meet-up. At the time, there was a lot of talk about the Danish king having fathered a few illegitimate children in Iceland. Naturally, every girl wants to be a princess, and I have to admit that that rumour gave me a brief flash of hope ... Mum was so beautiful that you just never knew. But then when I looked in the mirror I knew that it was hopeless:

Many a princess was left in this land
by the king as he travelled around,
but I'm so like my father that all understand
His Highness my mum never found.

Dad didn't want me to take over the farm here at Ljótarstaðir. So much so that he even tried to get Fanney to dissuade me. His intentions were good, of course – he wanted a better fate for me. He was worried about the drudgery and isolation. That I would end up feeling as confined and lonesome as him, and that I would be overwhelmed by it all. But he didn't recognize that times had changed and the world was different.

Much later, I found out that my dad's attitude hadn't been my only obstacle; another relative had tried by every means possible to prevent me from taking over the farm. My family members are so unforthcoming that I wasn't told until much later. When I heard about it, I was absolutely furious. But there was little else to do then but calm down; that was in the past, and there was no use fretting over it.

I must say, however, that I'm strongly opposed to young people being pushed into farming and taking over the family farm out of some sense of duty. Life is far too short to do anything but what makes you happy. I had no obligation to take over, and I wasn't pressured into it. Quite the opposite: the hurdles that I had to overcome were far greater than I could ever have predicted, and they grew even greater when Suðurorka began coveting my land.

My sisters and mum always supported my desire to take on the farm. I bought the land from Mum at a fair price, and my sisters gave me a part of their share. They sacrificed it gladly, because they wanted farming to continue here at Ljótarstaðir but weren't interested in taking over themselves; in other words, they backed me all the way. Ljótarstaðir is a heath farm, meaning that farming here can be so difficult, and there was every chance that any prospective buyer would have used it for something other than agriculture.

Ljótarstaðir is much more than a business and a home: it's also a place to which numerous people feel connected. My sisters didn't view the farm as a source of money, because they see things the same way I do. They and Mum are great conservationists and have supported the fight against the construction of power plants in the countryside and on our land from the very start. Nor am I interested in the money: in selling off my land in order to have an easier life.

When Dad got cancer in 2004, he had to undergo chemotherapy. He was so strong that at first the treatments didn't have any negative effects, and he continued working as he'd always done. His hips and back were bad, as with so many farmers his age who'd been hauling everything around all their lives, hay and what have you. Otherwise, he was as healthy as can be. But in the autumn of 2006, the disease suddenly caught up with him.

That spring, I'd taken over ownership of the farm, with sheep, a quota and all the rest, signing the purchase agreement on my birthday in April. The business side of things immediately improved when everything came under one roof, so to speak, rather than being divided between me and Mum as it had been before.

One of my big plans was the thorough renovation of the farmhouse. I started that project in 2007 and finished it five years later, ending with the laundry room. It has made a huge difference. Every time I take a shower now, I'm still grateful for how much better and cleaner the facilities are.

I like building things. It's soothing. I've always had a hammer and nails at hand, as far back as I remember. But all those renovations and additions at Ljótarstaðir aren't the work of one person. That would have been impossible. Besides my mainstays, Siggeir and Fanney, my Aunt Birna and her son have often been here and helped me a great deal. One of the things that I built for my own pleasure after I took over the farm is the deck that runs around the house. But the way things are going, it looks as though it'll be some time before I get a chance to do any sunbathing there.

HEIÐA AT A POETRY MEET-UP

Talking about the sun deck at my house reminds me of a conversation I had with my sister Ásta two years ago, when we recalled how our Aunt Jóna repeatedly warned me about the dangers of fooling around on the newly built deck, because Google Earth was always trying to capture photos of such things. I really thought that Jóna was bullshitting and had started seeing perverts in every corner, until last summer, when I got a text message from Ásta while I was happily mowing my western hayfield. The message stated, simply: 'The Google car is in Skaftártunga, I swear.' I kept a weather eye on the farmhouse and not long afterwards, what do you know, the Google car drove up, and when the driver acted more than a little peculiarly, I sent Ásta and Jóna the following verse:

> Vexed I was with Google's car
> and its grinning driver's face,
> for racy pics he went too far –
> the bastard snuck towards my place.

HEIÐA THE POLICE OFFICER

I've tried all kinds of things. In 2004, I applied to become a district police officer here in the east. I did patrol shifts and radar speed enforcement, and worked security at public events.

The two-year course at the Police Academy really appealed to me. It included demanding physical training and strict discipline. In addition, trainees have to learn self-defence and grappling holds. I'd been accepted on the course and was on my way to start it . . . Dad had agreed to do the feeding for me that winter, but then he was diagnosed with cancer and I had to abandon my plan.

It was the usual story, my tendency to carry the weight of the world on my shoulders, that made me want to be a cop. I also needed another paying job that was more compatible with my farming and pregnancy scanning of ewes. My teaching job in Kirkjubæjarklaustur was wearing thin for me. I felt guilty when I was at home – for being so poorly prepared for my teaching – and guilty in the classroom, for not being at home doing the farm work.

I loved working with professional police officers. They were so good at dealing with people and defusing difficult situations, particularly calming down individuals who were freaking out.

Let me give you an example. The most terrified I've ever been in my life was on an emergency response to a fight at a motorbike enthusiasts' dance in Kirkjubæjarklaustur. There were loads of people at the dance, so we were joined by reinforcements from Reykjavik, along with special forces. As we drove into the parking lot, the venue's double door opened and the crowd tumbled out, head over heels, raring for a fight. I thought: what in the devil's name am I doing here? I'll be killed.

I knew no defensive holds and hadn't yet undergone any police training. I've never wanted so much to turn on my heels and run as when I saw that avalanche of brawling bikers. My heart was beating so fast I thought I was going to have a coronary. But I stayed with the other cops rushing into the throng and started trying to calm people down. It went pretty well, and the situation was swiftly defused despite it looking so bad at the start.

But once almost everyone had left, a highly agitated fellow wielding a shovel came rushing towards me and the other cops. One smallish officer, an extremely tough customer, just glared at him so ferociously, baton raised, that the shovel-wielding fellow cowered and scrammed. The officer's glare was so fierce that even I felt frightened by him. And the fight concluded with the instigator, the one who'd been most riled, picking a marigold from a nearby flowerbed and presenting it to me.

It was such a positive experience being on the police force, even if I knew nothing compared to my fellow officers. Truly character-building. I could seriously imagine becoming a cop, perhaps a patrol officer. But then again something I've always struggled with is taking things too much to heart, so I don't think that I would have coped well with some cases, such as those involving domestic violence.

FÍFILL

I got a German Shepherd puppy from Stokkseyri last autumn. I went and chose the little chap when he was two weeks old. Then I brought him home when he was eight weeks old. It isn't good to bring home puppies younger than that. I was so excited to get him that I visited him twice in the meantime.

After meeting Kleó, Adda from Herjólfsstaðir's old Shepherd bitch, I knew that I wanted a Shepherd for myself. Adda had heard about some puppies on the way at Gunnarsholt Breeders and she'd decided to get one. There was one female in the litter, Rökkva (Dusky), and Adda chose her. Adda knew how much I wanted a Shepherd, so she encouraged me to get a puppy from the same litter and promised to help, this being such new territory for me.

Since then, I've often wondered if I've bitten off more than I can chew. I don't know if I'll have the time to train this dog. And besides, he's going to be massive. I'll have to slaughter whole rams to keep him fed. At least here in the countryside there are always enough scraps of meat that are good for boiling and feeding to the dogs.

It's hard work raising this breed because it's so special. A lot can go wrong if you're not careful. Shepherds have both gentle temperaments and guard-dog instincts. They're tender and sensitive. It's very easy to ruin them. If you're too authoritarian, they can become difficult. They need enormous affection and attention. These dogs mustn't be too tough: you absolutely can't end up with a dog that's aggressive. And they have to be completely obedient. So it's a real challenge to train this breed. On top of everything else, as Fífill grew bigger he started snoring like a trawlerman.

But it's so incredibly good to have him – he's my ghostbuster. Now he's started sleeping in a crate by my bed. Dogs prefer sleeping in crates at night. Fífill goes mad with happiness as soon as I start stirring in the morning. But he's so considerate that he keeps quiet if I stop moving and doze off again.

After I got him, Fífill stayed with Fanney in Hveragerði for the six weeks that I was doing pregnancy scanning. The master of the house naturally needs to be the boss, and there's a risk that a puppy will start looking to an older dog as the boss if its master is away. And then it can all go wrong.

Staying with Fanney was so good for Fífill as he needs to feel at home in an urban environment too; he can't be like some hick country dog that's never been away from the farm. Fanney took him to the dog park, where he hung out with all sorts of other dogs, which made him better adjusted. He became accustomed to seeing young people and old, cyclists, people in wheelchairs, just as all dogs ought to do.

AT LJÓTARSTAÐIR, 22 JUNE

The group of lambs by the sheep-house are bottle lambs. There are ten of them, and I've never had so many at once. We feed them three times a day, so we deliberately taught them to drink from buckets instead of sucking from bottles, and now just buckets will do. It saves us a lot of work.

Look, there's Blindigaur (Blind Guy). He's a blind yearling, a bottle lamb from last year that I couldn't bring myself to put down. He's not exactly the pride of the farm. He's the first lamb that visitors here see, and has such a whiny bleat, the poor thing, panning his head like a sheep with a cystic brain lesion. He's been kept all on his own here on the home hayfield for the last few days. When he got to meet the other lambs again this morning, he was so happy.

SIGGEIR

I'm just back from a trip to the Faroe Islands, to which Fanney and I invited Siggeir Ásgeirsson from Framnes in Mýrdalur in honour of his eightieth birthday. Sometimes I secretly call Siggeir my foster father, you know, when no one can hear me. It has nothing to do with my mother, it's just that over the years he's slowly become a father figure to me. Not only that, but Siggeir has also had to put up with Fanney and me calling him our brother every now and then; he joins in the game, and the three of us pretend we're siblings. Well, what else would you expect, with both our fathers being named Ásgeir?

Siggeir is an old friend of the family at Ljótarstaðir. He has always been there for me with advice and encouragement. There's no more beautiful soul to be found on this earth. He's so kind, always laughing and light-hearted. As a kid, I was particularly attached to him. He had a way of never belittling me, as I sometimes felt others did. I often think about what a great responsibility dealing with children is.

Siggeir can turn his hand to just about everything. A few years ago he built a beautiful, old-style, turf-roofed gable farm at Framnes for himself and his sister. It's such a pleasure to visit them there at their well-kept farm.

We went for long, long walks in the Faroe Islands. It's wonderful to get to be outside on sunny summer days. That's something that I often miss out on thanks to all my tractor work, which is heaviest in the times of sunshine and good weather. But I always enjoy summer and its wonderful sunlight in my own way.

NEAR THE TOP OF THE BALLOT

I was gobsmacked when Mum told me the other day that a woman had called to propose that I take one of the top places on the list of candidates for the Left-Green Movement in the Southern Constituency in the elections this autumn. The woman said that an electoral list was being put together and the decision had been made to ask me to add my name to it. The woman had called at nine in the evening, but I was already in bed. She was puzzled until it was explained to her that we were on lambing schedule – then it clicked.

My sister Stella was here when this happened, as well as María, Fanney's daughter. They were practically rolling on the floor with laughter. It was the joke of the week. So when the poor woman called again, I asked her flat out if this was a wind-up, but she just said no, so it wasn't a joke after all. We talked a bit and she said that the selection committee would contact me if I was open to the idea.

I was fertilizing the fields at Svínadalur – an abandoned farm whose hayfields I'm allowed to use – when the call came, and sure enough, they're deadly serious about this. I'm not being offered the position, but I wouldn't want that anyway. It's a pretty high one though, with a real chance of a parliamentary seat.

I don't know what to think. Yes, it could be fun to have a different job, if I did manage to get into parliament. But that's easier said than done. For instance, there's Mum. She had a stroke in 2013, and last winter she was hospitalized for three months with an infection in her knee. But now she's well enough to do cooking and knitting again. I don't want to be away from her for that long.

If I got into parliament, I would have to restructure the farm operations, and would of course have to hire someone to do most of the work. The thought of sitting on my butt all day thumbing through papers isn't entirely appealing either. It's also a real meat grinder: however hard they work, MPs never do a good enough job. And then there's the personal mud slinging. Do I really want to deal with that? There's the election process itself. Putting myself out there, promising 'Here I am! And this is what I'm going to do!' It's not really my style. And it's hardly what you'd expect from someone from Skaftafell either! And then after putting a huge amount of time and effort into the campaign, it could all come to nothing.

Of course, being an MP would be a big, important job – a challenge that's completely different from anything I've done so far, an entirely different scenario. I still have a lot of wanderlust and this stirs up the old gypsy in me, the longing to ramble and take on new tasks and experiences.

One of the things that make me hesitate is the fear of others trying to turn me into something that I'm not. I don't like sitting in meetings; I get restless and fidgety, lose focus quickly. I'm worried that I wouldn't have the patience to familiarize myself thoroughly with the issues, and would be ill-prepared.

Yes, I'm thinking it over – on my own. I don't feel like calling up all over the place, asking for opinions and advice on whether to do it. I'm always on my own anyway. And after all, the final decision has to be mine and mine alone.

It's true that I have difficulty performing in public. I've long had a dread of standing up in front of people, which gives me the shakes, and at its worst I lose my appetite. But that's also why this candidacy would be such an exciting challenge, as it's the best possible opportunity to overcome this fear! You might say that people are their own worst enemies, always pushing themselves to the extreme. I've done that all my life.

The idea of standing for election shows just how big the fight against the Búland Power Plant has become, because that's why I've been contacted. Clearly many people have been following this matter.

These kinds of projects really have to stop. That some dude in Reykjavik can just decide to build a power plant wherever he feels like it and start throwing money around to make it happen. It's an impossible system, when any old idea for a power plant should automatically go through a consultation process. The rules concerning these things are wrong. Our communities shouldn't have to be dragged through such processes.

Take Svartá in Bárðardalur. One of the two Halldórsstaðir farms there has pulled out of its agreement with the energy firm that was going to construct the plant. That's a huge development. The farmers realized that the proposed power plant was a much bigger project, capable of far greater detrimental effects, than they'd thought, so they terminated the agreement. I can really understand how difficult a decision that must have been for them, considering everything I've been through. It isn't fair to drag people into such madness. It's bullying of the worst sort.

HEIÐA AT A PUBLIC MEETING

People know what's going on even if they aren't making a lot of noise about it; folk from Skaftafell are generally a reserved bunch, but now we're all scared, feeling threatened in a big way. One by one, people are standing up and saying 'But what about the Tungufljót River? We can't let them take away our Fljót, we *mustn't* let them take away our Fljót.' The most unlikely people have now begun declaring publicly that Fljót is a gem of nature. They're right, it's unique: incredibly beautiful and packed with fish and bird life. It's also our chief landmark and, after all, how are we who live 'beyond Fljót' supposed to complain about the laziness of those living 'east of Fljót' – and vice versa, of course – if there's no Fljót any more? The thought of it is shaking our community to its foundations.

Even Sigfús, the farmer at Borgarfell, who never stops working except maybe on Christmas Eve or when it's one of his kids' birthdays, has started suggesting that he could take people on guided tours, one group of hikers each summer along Fljót, if that would help to

support the cause. In short, we're worried, good people
– really worried.

It would be strange to stand for election and possibly
get into parliament when I've always been such a harsh
critic of our party system. I find it terribly corrupt –
don't even get me started on the partisan scheming of
the MPs. In becoming one of them, I'd have to start
pushing for this and that issue all the time. So what am
I doing thinking of joining such a screwed-up system? I
don't know, but maybe I could do some good despite
my partisan interests. Maybe it could work, with a lot
of squabbling and stubbornness. But do I really want to
bother?

I don't know whether I could stay focused. Or if I
would start suddenly writing a poem or thinking of
different ways to organize lambing in the middle of an
official meeting. Trying my best to look intelligent while
not having a clue as to what's going on. It wouldn't be
good to find myself fumbling for a rhyme in the third
verse while important matters were being discussed.
I'm already bad at preventing my mind from drifting in
meetings; I start making up stories and wondering
about things. If a speaker is extra boring, my mind goes
off on tangents: how can anyone be this dull? Is he
from the Stone Age? Is this man a mummy?

As far as a possible job in parliament goes, I have it
on good authority from my friend Þór Saari, who's been
an MP, that it would drive me mad. I'm used to jobs
that I can dive into, tackle head on and solve. It doesn't

work like that in the Alþingi and the Icelandic government in general, where everything happens at a snail's
pace. That would probably be the greatest trial, hearing
nothing about certain matters for weeks and months.

Þór even wrote a book entitled *What's Wrong with
this Alþingi?* His book makes it all sound so awful. I
got furious reading it. The way things are done! For
example, he'd just finished helping his daughter with
her homework one evening and was checking his
email, when by chance he found an important bill due
to be voted on the next day. In other words, bills are
dumped on MPs with such short notice that they don't
have sufficient time to read them unless they pull all-
nighters. As if people's brains function properly at
night!

The Alþingi is a very unique workplace. Þór Saari
says that being an MP was the worst, most wearisome
job he'd ever had. It doesn't sound the most appealing
of prospects . . . and it seems as if the MPs just give up
and stop bothering to do their work with the necessary
care.

23 JUNE

I'm under a lot of time pressure now because of my holiday in the Faroe Islands. It wasn't the most sensible thing to take such a break, not with the amount of work I've got piled on my shoulders. I'm late with my soil cultivation. I should have been finished sowing by now. I'll have to plough as long into the night as I can last (I started at six this morning). Then I need to finish cultivating. This isn't helped by my using equipment borrowed from the Agricultural Society, as I can't organize things as I normally would or start when I want to. Once I'm done ploughing and cultivating, I need to sow and smooth the soil. There's a lot of winterkill in the fields this summer. I need to take one field that's in very poor shape and rework it, while resting another tilled area from last year.

But it's no use being stressed. I just need to get on with it. Get the seeds into the ground. Get the sheep up into the mountains. Luckily I've finished with the clean-up after lambing. I would have liked to have finished oiling the deck as well, the sheep corral and the fences, but I still have all of that left to do. Mum has always been a great help with such things in the past, but it's a lot more difficult for her now because of her bad leg.

It's not all work, though. On Saturday I'm going to Reykjavik to help my Uncle Addi turn fifty. And then I'm going to Andri Snær's election party. He's definitely my favourite candidate. Otherwise, I could almost vote for Elísabet Jökulsdóttir. I like her slogan: 'More fun!'

I work long days in the endless midsummer light, and sometimes I have to work at night, too.

In my first years running the farm, I worked and worked and worked all day and all night. I feel exhausted just thinking about it. Once I went completely bonkers; I don't know how many nights straight I'd been working. I was still ploughing and it was near dawn. Then I started seeing all sorts of things coming up from the soil. Cows appeared and sheep appeared. When I saw a fertilizer spreader emerge from the soil I shut off the tractor. The fertilizer spreader was blue.

I've stopped working as hard as that. I don't even try to work several nights in a row any more. When I get a Snapchat at a ridiculous hour from my young cousins out in the countryside who are working as I was, I just think to myself: you little monkeys, you'll only be able to do that for a few more years and then that'll be it!

Most often these days, I go to bed at a reasonable hour and just wake up really early. Working non-stop is long, long in the past.

The interesting thing is that even though I don't work such long hours any more, I'm actually more productive. This has come with experience and maturity. Sometimes in the past I complicated things so much that I'm sure I did more damage than good. Now I've optimized our facilities and conditions so well that a lot of tasks take much less time and effort. The contrast between then and now is like night and day. The greatest improvements have been to the sheep-houses. And my equipment is much better, too.

25 JUNE

All that said, this is the third night in a row now I've been ploughing and cultivating. I've slept for just four hours each night. I'm not that tired, but now my body is very stiff from sitting in the tractor for so long. Which isn't healthy, of course. Today I'll be cultivating until past noon, and then I'll go with Mum to vote in the presidential elections in Kirkjubæjarklaustur. Then I need to hurry to Reykjavik for Addi's birthday and Andri Snær's election party. The sowing is going to have to wait until I return.

AT LJÓTARSTAÐIR, 26 JUNE

I just got home now, around dinnertime. We were the last to leave the bar in Reykjavik, around five this morning.

I got up at the crack of dawn yesterday, thinking it would only take me about three hours to cultivate what was left, but it ended up taking me five. Then there were phone calls and more phone calls, and time just ticked away.

I hadn't taken a shower for three days because my sleep time, those four hours a night, was far too precious to waste on anything as unnecessary as a shower. By yesterday I was so dirty I thought I might block the drain; the shower floor was covered with mud. My hair was knotted and full of dirt, and I stank of stale sweat and dust. Please note that this is not usual. Under normal circumstances, I do myself the honour of bathing regularly, even if I have no reason to leave the farm.

Then Mum and I drove to Klaustur to vote, even though I hadn't had time to brush my hair. Then I brought Mum home to Ljótarstaðir and drove on to Reykjavik. I changed clothes at Fanney's place in

Hveragerði. I actually put on a dress: incredibly chic. I looked as if I'd never been in a tractor.

The special cocktail on offer at Addi's birthday party was vodka with orange juice – 'a screwdriver' – which is of course an orange-coloured drink, but Fanney had added some blue food colouring – organic, mind you – and turned it green as grass. Now it was a special eco-warrior drink. She mixed it in her finest glass carafe with a spout, which we'd hauled back with us from the Faroe Islands. Also served were huge sandwich cakes made by Kolla – more than enough for both the party *and* breakfast the next day.

Speaking of the green eco-warrior drink, Addi is another conservationist, like so many of my relatives, though he's no fanatic. My sisters, my mum and I are opposed to the Búland Power Plant. And most of our relatives don't want to see me overrun, either, even though they aren't necessarily opposed to power plants in general. But as far as the exploitation of natural resources is concerned, I want us all to stop for a moment and think. I'm entirely opposed to Iceland's continued construction of power plants at the expense of the environment.

Uncle Addi is my go-to repairman. He takes care of anything related to my electrical systems; I'm terribly afraid of fire, and consequently terrified of electricity. Addi installed new lights in all the farm buildings, which makes a huge difference in the winter darkness. He also gives me advice about phone and computer purchases. He has amazing patience with his problem niece, who calls him at all hours with annoying questions. He's always running errands for me in Reykjavik too, buying whatever it is I might need or taking things in for repair.

Anyway, after the birthday party, Fanney, Drífa and I went downtown, to Andri Snær's election party. I said hello and told him that I was a staunch supporter of his. It was clear then that Andri wouldn't be the next president of Iceland. I try not to think about how Iceland missed the chance to elect this man; it saddens me that we didn't all rally around Andri. It was great that he stood though, because it meant that the focus of the presidential election shifted more toward environmental conservation and climate change.

After the election party at Iðnó, around one o'clock, we went to the Icelandic Bar: I'm not sure if it's the one right by the National Theatre, as I don't really know my way around the city. Then we carried on to Vegamót, then to Lebowski and then to the gay bar, Kiki. If you go out in Reykjavik, you might as well do it right!

We gave the beer Einstök (Unique) a new name: now it's called Mistök (Mistake). Normally, though, I don't drink beer; on such expeditions, I prefer vodka with orange juice and a few shots, just whatever happens to be pouring, really – although I can't say I'm a fan of rain downpours or emotional outpours!

This particular drinking expedition ended up cheaper than usual because of how little sleep I'd had ploughing and cultivating for almost three days straight, but I still had a blast. I knew it would be fun, especially because I hadn't seen Drífa for so long. She's a real party animal and a fantastic person. She studied psychology and criminology in Britain and is currently writing a doctorate, developing her thesis for calculating the basic social costs of domestic violence. We've been friends for over twenty years now.

We had such a great night. Drífa claims that men fluttered around me like moths drawn to light. That figures, me being such a goddamn lamppost. In any case, I didn't notice the swarm that Drífa claims to have seen and I just enjoyed myself without distractions.

Drífa is also a mixed martial arts competitor with the club Mjölnir. I have absolutely no chance of beating her now, but when I was at Norður-Hvammur, we were more evenly matched and used to knock each other around her little wooden farmhouse . . . and there were times when we could easily have kicked each other through the wall. But her mother was so annoyed by our roughness that she banished us from the house, telling us that we were behaving like crazy stallions.

Drífa is determined to push me into standing for election. When I said that I was worried about being turned into something that I'm not, she told me to stop being a wimp and punched me hard in the stomach. Luckily, I managed to tense up before the punch, so it wasn't that bad.

At the next bar, I'd become tired of her playing with her phone and sending text messages all the time, so I started trying to grab it. She told me to stop being a jerk and then, using a takedown technique that she'd conveniently just learned at Mjölnir, she suddenly flipped me onto the floor. With me in a dress! Her as well! And there I lay, until she yanked me up and said: 'Now we stop! The both of us!'

Activism is in Drífa's blood. Her dad Jónas was instrumental in preventing the construction of an aluminium smelter in Dyrhólaey and Dyrhólahöfn in 1974. That sort of absurdity would never cross anyone's mind now, all due to Jónas. He called me today, and we talked for an hour. He, too, was encouraging me to stand for election.

I don't feel bad at all today. After partying, I sometimes feel a bit tired, but I'm never hungover. Headache. Stomach ache. Hangover. I never get them. My sisters are like that too; just another hereditary thing I guess.

AT LJÓTARSTAÐIR, 27 JUNE

No, I'm not going to watch the football match between England and Iceland tonight. I don't have time.

Things here went south this morning when the tractor malfunctioned. It wouldn't start. So I hopped on my quad bike and herded a few sheep up onto the heath instead, since I'd received permission to do so from the Soil Conservation Service. We at Ljótarstaðir and Snæbýli are closest to the highland pastures, so we don't have to spend time and effort carting sheep up in trailers.

While I was herding the sheep, Palli from Hvammur repaired the tractor. I'd already mixed the rapeseed in with the fertilizer, and had finished spreading one sackful when the fertilizer spreader broke. I was sowing rapeseed so that the lambs would have more than just grass to graze on in the autumn. Palli fixed everything up, brought his fertilizer spreader, finished sowing the rapeseed and fertilized the other tilled area. He doesn't trust himself to sow it with his fertilizer spreader, so another neighbour will come this evening and do the job for me with a seeder.

Then the frame of the fertilizer spreader broke, tearing an axle out of the transmission. It's seriously damaged and will need a huge amount of repair work, including welding. I'll have to hoist it into the back of my old Lux and take it down to Álftaver for repairs. Typical – just when I go to use something, it breaks. The spreader is nine years old, and also broke down last year; it's been a real bloody pain.

It isn't that difficult to operate any of these machines. Ploughing is the trickiest: the plough needs to be straight behind the tractor, so it has to be set correctly. None of this is any big deal if you're used to working with such equipment. But of course it's stressful when the equipment breaks down. A lot of farmers are brilliant at being able to do everything and fix anything. I can change filters, but that's about as far as it goes.

Now all I have left to do is level the fields. I share a land roller with three other farmers. The roller pushes down the seeds so they germinate sooner, and there's less chance of it all going to pot if the wind starts blowing. I'm late with this because of my holiday, but if this good weather lasts, everything will be fine.

My sister Stella, who lives in Akureyri, came for a short visit, on her way to her daughter Arndís's place at Meðalland. I just managed to have a quick lunch with her and Arndís and the grandkids. But as usual, I'm pressed for time. Now it's all about finishing the field work, releasing the sheep, getting the haymaking equipment ready and the fertilizer spreader repaired. There's also loads of urgent maintenance work that needs doing, including replacing the corrugated iron roofing on Rimma, my second sheep-house, oiling all the wood-work and fixing it up.

HAYMAKING AND ORGANIZATION

I'm an organizational freak. I always have plan A, B and C. I also have haymaking completely plotted out and organized. I'm going to mow at this o'clock, rake at that o'clock. Sudden rain drives me mad . . . just, how could this happen? Now all my careful scheduling is ruined. During my most hot-tempered years, whenever the weather wrecked my schedule I had to try to calm myself down by taking a shower. Now all I need is what works for those who've progressed a bit further down the path to maturity: a cup of coffee and a few choice swear words.

Over the last few summers, I've also gathered hay at the abandoned farm Svínadalur, around fifteen kilometres from here. It's going to involve a lot more work this summer because the fields there were so badly frost-damaged that I'll have to get more hay from elsewhere. So I'll also be doing haymaking at Holt in Síða. It'll take me an enormous amount of time to get there because the bridge over Eldvatn at Ási has been closed to all but passenger cars following the huge glacial flood in the Skaftá River. I'll have to cross Hrífunes heath, on the old highway, which is a much longer and more difficult route. And the side road to Holt isn't good either. It's a two-hour drive by tractor each way.

Haymaking doesn't take too long under ordinary circumstances, but the workload is heavy. And it isn't finished once the bales are made, because they can't be left out on the fields. You've got to gather them quickly and stack them, or seagulls can get to them, among other things. If there are holes in the plastic, the hay can become dangerous. If it becomes mouldy it will make the sheep sick from fodder poisoning.

It's sometimes said that farming *is* haymaking because it depends so heavily on harvesting good hay, and enough of it. Sadly, the workload involved in haymaking and my local politics and committee work for Vatnajökull National Park do not go particularly well together. It's impossible for me to say that I can attend a meeting or join in an excursion on this or that date much in advance. I've got to get my hay in. Period. Once or twice I've had to ask others to take over for me at the farm on a key day during haymaking when I simply couldn't get out of having to be somewhere else.

ELLA AND HEIÐA

Having my friend Ella from Úthlíð so close by has been a great support. We met at a Christmas dance when we were three years old. Mum says that we clicked instantly. We both started farming around the same time and have always helped each other out. We were often together at school, too, from boarding school in Klaustur to farmers' college in Hvanneyri. Over the years, Ella and I have made up a few maxims that we like to use at appropriate times.

If you're working at it, it'll work.

That is, even if it goes slowly, you'll succeed if you stick to your task. I'm pretty persistent. I can work in bursts, with breaks in between, but in general, I do things slowly but surely.

There's no hay without mowing.

This came to us once when the hay got wet. Naturally, you do a lot of mowing when the outlook's touch-and-go.

If you want the grass to turn green, you've got to open the fertilizer sacks.

Ella said this to me once after I'd fertilized the fields. Afterwards a cold spell came, and I wondered whether

I'd made a mistake, whether maybe it hadn't been the right time to do so.

Ella has a very large farm with both cows and sheep, and makes as much in a month as I do in a year. She bought her sheep from her parents when she took over the farm, and is now the majority owner in a company in charge of the entire operation.

She's a superwoman. She's twice as fast as me, and does everything twice as well. In round-ups, she's tireless – and she's super slim, nothing but sinew, muscle and bone. She has always been exceptionally hardworking, a real toughie. She was already helping deliver lambs when she was just a tot, and riding horses as well. My dad really liked her. He gave her a foal as a gift on her confirmation. Unfortunately, it turned out to be a damned lazy nag, but there was no way of knowing that beforehand. The thought behind the gift was nice, anyway.

Ella has sheep breeding in her blood, giving her the ability to achieve maximum returns from her flock. She has a good memory for lineages and knows each and every one of her sheep, something that I can't boast.

As far as breeding goes, I have a really hard time slaughtering mouflon gimmers. I just find them so beautiful. Added to which, sometimes I forget about inferior sheep. Sometimes it's happened that for the third spring in a row, I suddenly realize that a pretty poor sheep is still around! I don't have it in me to pore over flock registers to try to come up with ways to maximize my returns. Well, it's not that drastic; I've borrowed a ram or two from Ella and other farmers, of course, and will continue to do so. Otherwise, I've accepted the fact that this is how I am. I take excellent care of my animals. Their well-being is very important to me; I know how they're doing, and I enjoy being with them, too. If I go for a few days without petting an animal, I start to feel like something's missing.

My favourite sheep colour is mouflon, called *golóttur* around here, but *botnóttur* most everywhere else. It's when the sheep has a white belly but is dark on top. When it's white at the throat and rump. White inside the ears. White eyebrows. In other words, it's white at both ends, and underneath. On top it can be black, or grey. Most common is black. To be really pretty, they need to be really dark.

I only have two brown mouflons now, and an embarrassingly large number of black mouflons. Then there are the grey ones, called *grágolóttar*. Elsewhere, they'd be called *grábotnóttar* (grey mouflon) and *móbotnóttar* (brown mouflon), or even *mórubotnóttar* (moorit mouflon). In some places in the Westfjords they're called *gofóttar*. That sounds a bit like *kofa* – *lundakofa* – a puffin chick; and puffins are of course mouflon-patterned with white bellies and black backs. Now I'm just playing around, taking wild stabs at where the name comes from.

CANDIDACY AND HAYMAKING ON AN UNFAMILIAR FIELD, 4 JULY

I got here around three, and will be finished around midnight. The weather is nice, though there was a shower earlier. It only rained here, nowhere else. Typical! I noticed that my neighbours at Hunkubakkar had already finished mowing and were gathering in the bales. But rain doesn't matter so much when you're mowing.

I'm unfamiliar with the fields here, so I daren't go full throttle. I'm driving carefully, a bit hesitantly – also because the grass is so high – or I might end up in a ditch. It helps, though, that I've done some raking here for my neighbour before, so I have a slight idea of the lie of the land.

I've rolled fifty bales at home at Ljótarstaðir, so that's a start.

Yesterday I was called and asked officially to take the second place on the list for the Left-Green Movement in the Southern Constituency. So it looks like I'm going for it. Now I'm preparing for my candidacy and informing my colleagues on the municipal council of my decision. I'm still not sure I'm doing the right thing, but I know that I would be even more disgruntled if I didn't go for it. It's better to put yourself out there than do nothing. But this isn't a simple decision. I'm the kind of person who prefers the peace and quiet of home.

Jesus, there went a duck! I hope I haven't driven over its nest. No, there it is. I missed it, thank goodness. I count eight eggs in the nest. There are birds everywhere here. I'm constantly moving snipe chicks out of the uncut grass.

This candidacy of mine reminds me of when I became a professional and a competitive sheep shearer. I went for these to see if I could handle them, if I was tough enough, if my back was strong enough. Both this candidacy and shearing in its various forms are a real challenge.

Oh, what were the people who made this field thinking? My tractor keeps taking off every time it hits one of the plough furrows here!

It would of course be terrible if we didn't get someone elected from the Southern Constituency; if things went exactly like last time. Naturally, though, I'll do my best so that I and the candidate in first place on the list both get in. If I'm going to go for it, I want to get all the way to parliament.

Oof, I'm getting lost in this field. I can't see anything in this tall grass. I'm in the weeds, literally. But it'll be okay. I've got a hyperactive guardian angel who ensures that I make it through things in one piece – mostly.

MORE HAYMAKING
AT HOLT, 5 JULY

I nabbed a few hours' sleep, finished mowing around half past midnight, then made one luggage trip for the Hiking Association this morning and was back here at noon for tedding. Arriving any earlier wouldn't have helped because it rained this morning.

I don't have to pay for the use of the fields here at Holt. The owners are just glad that they're being mown. The grass is good, and there's a lot of it. I'll probably end up with around two hundred bales. But it'll be very expensive haymaking because I have to drive the tractor all this way, here and back, meaning I'm burning tons of fuel. It'll take quite a few trips altogether. And this off-farm haymaking is extremely time-consuming. But there's no use complaining – farming is haymaking. I'm only doing this because of the winterkill in my fields, and because the additional hay that I get from Svínadalur simply isn't enough.

Haymaking so far from home needs to be organized extremely well. The equipment has to be moved from one place to the other, in the right order: mower, tedder, hay rake, baler. I've got to ted now until seven o'clock;

it won't be possible later as that's when the dew sets in. Of course, I only have the tractor here, no car. At one point it looked as if I might have to camp here for the night. But no need, because my sister Fanney has to go to a meeting in Kirkjubæjarklaustur, so she'll drive me home to Ljótarstaðir.

A PHONE CALL, 17 JULY

Now I'm at Svínadalur doing some mowing. The weather's damp, but it's better just to go for it than sit on your hands. I haven't heard anything more about my possible candidacy. Things feel uncertain at this point.

I had excellent help finishing the haymaking at Holt. My nephew Ármann, from Ásar in Skaftártunga, brought his truck. We used my Grey at Holt to load the hay into the truck, and borrowed a John Deere tractor from my neighbours at Gröf to unload it at home. Ármann is an absolute workhorse. We moved the bales at night; there's no way you can be on the roads during the day with heavy loads, there's so much traffic. Holt is on the same side road as the hugely popular Fjaðrárgljúfur Canyon. We made four trips, and neither of us slept a wink that night. But it was easy for me, since Ármann did all the driving.

Then I brought the last bales from Holt home using my wagon, which naturally took some time to load. When I reached Gröf, just before Ljótarstaðir, who should have overtaken me but Ármann, who was transporting sheep to the highland pastures. He'd just had a cup of coffee before getting on with it – while I went home and went to bed. It was a good feeling to be home again with that big batch of hay.

Just to be clear: off-farm haymaking, like I do in Holt, and haymaking in general, is never a one-person job. That would be impossible.

19 JULY

I'm driving the hay bales home from Svínadalur. Each trip takes three hours, but that seems really short after my Holt adventure. The road is bad the last stretch up to this abandoned farm, as are the hayfield paths, so it's taking a while.

Mowing was touch-and-go, and I was lucky to gather the hay so quickly. Often you've just got to seize the moment.

Haymaking is going extremely well this summer. I have around thirty-five hectares left to mow at home. They're the fields that I use for grazing the sheep, so they wouldn't have been ready for mowing until now, even if I hadn't had to deal with the winterkill problem.

NOON, 21 JULY

I'm on my way out after lunch. I had visitors who stayed for a long time yesterday – I thought they'd be here for an hour, but they arrived at four o'clock and left at half past eleven. It was Steinar Kaldal of the Icelandic Environment Association and a British TV crew that he was showing around. They're making a film about Iceland's central highlands. They asked me so many questions, and had me answer in Icelandic, even though the questions were in English. My English is okay, but it's better in such situations to be allowed to speak Icelandic instead of having to fumble for the right word. Icelandic has just the right words for what needs to be said in this regard.

When I'm not haymaking in the summer, I use the time for maintenance work, such as painting the farm buildings. There were big projects going on here in the summers of 2013 and 2014 – we replaced the iron on the roofs where it was needed, and painted all of them. That second autumn, I didn't think I would finish all the painting before I had to go and round up the sheep for winter. But Mum and I just managed to splash the last bit of paint onto the final walls before I left. I'd had some help with the painting before, and when Fanney came, we worked hard on it together.

I'd been racking my brain over colour samples from Harpa. I have a relative who works there, and they sent me little tester pots. I eventually decided on royal blue and I'm very happy with it. It's always a special feeling when I'm driving home and catch a glimpse of my beautiful blue roofs.

Another summer maintenance job is spraying the farmhouse with a high-pressure washer, to keep the cladding clean. Call me fussy. At least I am when I park the hay wagon, the tedder, the machinery in general – it's all always lined up at an obsessive ninety-degree angle to my house.

FESTIVAL IN THE WESTMANN ISLANDS, 3 AUGUST

I had a great time at the Workers' Weekend Festival, as always, even though this time I went on my own as Fanney couldn't come and Drífa cancelled at the last minute.

Fanney once lived in the Westmann Islands; she used to be a head teacher there. I'd stopped going to the festival before she moved to the Islands, and I wouldn't go now if I didn't have friends that I could stay with in town. Once you're an adult, you don't want to be staying in a tent on the festival grounds any more.

It's been wonderful to sort of grow up alongside this festival and I met a lot of people I know there. I find I'm always bumping into the same group of people, but somehow miss a load of others that I know are there somewhere. Of course, it's such a huge crowd, fifteen thousand people. Partying in the white tents with the locals is the key to having the best time. And I had so much fun that I didn't get back until eight on Monday morning.

4 AUGUST

The recent earthquakes are big, of course, but Katla gets restless at this time every year – and one of these years, she'll erupt for sure. It's also expected that Bárðarbunga will erupt again in the very near future. This year or next, says Ármann Höskuldsson, the vulcanologist. I'm trying to stay informed so I can react when the time comes, but it's impossible to live in this area and be continually stressed over the threat of a volcanic eruption. Life's too short. I wouldn't mind, though, if it were more than just twenty-five kilometres from Katla to Ljótarstaðir as the crow flies!

EXCURSION TO THE MOUNTAIN PASS, VONARSKARÐ, 12 AUGUST

Last Tuesday I had to participate in an excursion to Vonarskarð with the board of Vatnajökull National Park and the park rangers. I'd known about the trip for a long time, but the timing was awful, during haymaking – I can't plan for such things ahead of time. There's an insane amount of work that needs doing on the farm, but there was no way I could get out of the excursion because my deputy works in tourism and simply couldn't make it.

I'm chairman of the Western Regional Committee for Vatnajökull National Park. I care deeply about this park, and want to see it enlarged, but national parks aren't the favourite child of municipal councils and landowners in these parts. It took a great deal of wrangling with my municipal council to get its expansion (and the barest minimum of an expansion at that) approved. It wouldn't have gone through without the compromise of power-plant proposals remaining on the master plan, including the Búland Power Plant, which is practically in my backyard.

On Sunday I raked what I had left . . . thirty hectares. Yes, that's a lot of raking for one day.

Fanney and Siggeir drove my old Lux out here on Monday, carrying the corrugated iron sheets and felt for the roof of the sheep-house Rimma in a trailer. When they arrived, I was raking at Hvammur. The iron sheets weigh a ton and can only be moved with the tractor. I couldn't leave in Fanney's car until I'd taken them off the trailer. Then Fanney went and loaded up the trailer again, while Siggeir went to cut the grass around my farmhouse with his petrol mower; he's the farm's designated lawn mower. Afterwards, they brought building materials up to Hólaskjól to continue working there.

Fanney has a summer job with the angling association that runs the Highland Centre at Hólaskjól. She's the baggage driver and hut warden and paints and builds and goodness knows what else. Fanney and Siggeir drove up there in my old Lux, while I took her Old Red for the Vonarskarð trip. Good trade.

That evening I set off to Vonarskarð, taking Fífill with me in Fanney's Toyota Hilux, which has a covered bed, unlike mine.

We arrived at Nýidalur around three in the morning. Fífill was a little over-excited and I wanted to make sure that he didn't chew apart the car's interior if I left him alone. He wasn't allowed in the hut, so the two of us curled up in the car.

Before bedding down, we walked over to the outhouse – Fífill on his leash – and a tourist suddenly appeared out of the darkness. Fífill went ballistic at this unexpected encounter and started barking loudly, determined to protect his owner. The poor tourist was so frightened that he flattened himself against the outhouse wall, arms splayed to either side. I couldn't tell him that my huge dog was 'completely harmless,' because I couldn't get the creature to stop barking, however I tried. I even tried holding Fífill's mouth shut, but he just barked louder out of the corners of it.

We got up at seven that morning and set off on our trip around eight-thirty. It's such a unique area, with a spectacular view of the glacier and the liparite mountains. Snapadalur, that green valley in the barren terrain, then a geothermal area at 1,060 metres above sea level, lush vegetation blanketing a small patch where all sorts of different species thrive. It's incomparable.

The weather was very still and bright with perfect views in all directions . . . it's truly indescribable, seeing Hofsjökull Glacier, Nýidalur and the back side of Þvermóður ('Contrary'). This peak gets its name from the way that it sticks out from the surrounding mountains. For obvious reasons Þvermóður is a great favourite of mine, and I feel a definite kinship with it.

This area is full of monstrous monuments to past times in Iceland. Huge levees that the National Power Company of Iceland erected around 1970 in order to divert water southward from the sources of the Skjálfandafljót River, which runs northward; in other words, to divert a few tributaries to increase the volume of water flowing south. But after the first snowmelts, these tributaries just followed their old courses, and have done so ever since. The levees are so big, some as high as four or five metres, that they're visible on Google Earth. At the time, these and similar projects were undertaken without any sort of consultation process. No environmental impact assessment, nothing. Such impetuousness. The days of such arrogance ought to have been over and done with, and these sorts of assaults against nature things of the past.

The Þjórsá area is all more or less manmade now – the water is diverted from every accessible river and creek. There are all sorts of irrigation ditches and power-harnessing structures, and roads everywhere. But to come across those massive levees in the middle of the highlands – you just don't expect it.

That's how it used to be with road construction. Hey, isn't that a great slope for a road, someone would say, and then the bulldozer would drive up the slope – no, actually it isn't good enough . . . let's take this one instead. You can find these awful bulldozer tracks across so many places in the landscape. But at least the men and their machines don't behave like this any more.

The hike to Vonarskarð turned out to be twenty-five kilometres and Fífill was terribly tired. He looked on the verge of giving up, but held on and made it. It's all just rock there, so his paws were sore, but I checked him every now and then and saw that the pads hadn't cracked, which is just as well. He was so worn out that he slept in the tractor all the next day. He didn't want to leave it – just like an old dog.

As usual, I walked the whole way in my rubber shoes and wool socks, which astonished my fellow travellers in their hiking boots! And then I had such a good time. Rangers and the like are such great company, as are all people with jobs having to do with nature. It's so nice to get to hang out with such a group.

Fífill and I drove back that evening and got home around three in the morning, after one other brief adventure. On the road, I met a guide with a group of French tourists; a wheel on their luggage trailer had broken, so I drove their stuff out to Hrauneyjar for them. This added another hour or so to our trip back. It certainly came in handy that we were in Fanney's Hilux, with its covered bed.

17 AUGUST

Siggeir and I are repairing the lamb house, using old construction techniques. Building walls from rocks and turf is a great art, and Siggeir knows his stuff. We started at noon yesterday, will be at it all day today and hope to finish tomorrow. The walls had become skewed and were starting to fall apart. We used the same rocks, and also added some flagstones from the old farmhouse ruins to fill in the gaps. Nowadays you can use machinery for this sort of work to some extent: cut out and transport the turf using the tractor. This has to be finished by the autumn, and it'll be great to have the lamb house back in working order. The weather is excellent: twelve degrees and just a few showers. All this rock and turf is quite heavy, of course, so it's good that it isn't too warm outside.

Compared to Siggeir, I'm all thumbs and too impulsive. Every time I wreck something that he then has to fix – for instance, if I break a board or ruin a screw – he calls me a 'dreadful dub'. When I damaged the trailer brake valve on the drop-side trailer, he called me a dreadful dub. My neighbour Ingi from Snæbýli laughed out loud and added: 'I know . . . and what she doesn't trample underfoot, she hurls into the sky.'

I've got such a hot temper that it can take a great deal of effort for me to keep myself calm – usually with mixed results. If I'm stressed and feel pulled in too many directions at once, or if I'm having difficulty with a task, I get short-tempered. In such cases, I often grab whatever's handy and hurl it into the blue sky – a broom, a hammer – and I then have to go off and find it once I've cooled down. I also get impatient when working: if things don't go right, I can simply lose it. Then everyone's an idiot, and just in my way!

Fanney and María got me a pair of powerful binoculars for Christmas, which would come in handy during round-ups. They asked the man at the shop if the binoculars could survive being hurled into the blue. The poor man was apparently more than a bit perplexed by the question.

But my dogs and sheep don't suffer from my temper. It's reserved for inanimate objects. As proof, I can tell you about a French bulldog that was here for a while; he was kept inside the farmhouse and barked all day long. I told him over and over that I would knock his block off if he didn't keep his mouth shut. I never did it, though . . . and the creature never shut up.

HEIÐA ON THE BALLOT

Now it's all clear. I'm going to be listed second on the ballot for the Left-Green Movement in the Southern Constituency in the coming parliamentary election. It's pretty exciting, a great challenge of course; I fully realize that. It's impossible to refuse the chance to be in a position of influence in matters that are so important to me: environmental conservation, agriculture, equal rights of every sort – gender, people of all races, all religions.

For me, personally, this also has to do with my not wanting to die without having lived, with wanting to go for it and seize opportunities. This is an opportunity to live life to the fullest. Maybe it's a sign of my restlessness – my longing for something – to want more, to keep going, onward, as far as I can go.

Whether this is ambition, I don't know. I'm not familiar enough with that word to apply it to myself. It's more about pursuing the things that are close to my heart. I'm furious about the effects that the methods applied by big business have on ordinary people. This has to be stopped. One of my goals is to do something about this, to have an influence and draw attention to this type of bullying.

There's one thing, perhaps, that drives me most strongly: my loathing for the attitude of those who sit at their kitchen tables criticizing everything and everyone, who have the answers to everything but aren't willing to step up and do something about it. I don't want to remain sitting at that kitchen table.

All of us involved in this campaign are well aware of the fact that ours is a difficult constituency, full of Independent and Progressive Party supporters. And we'll just have to see how it goes.

There's not much chance of me making it into parliament. On the other hand, I've got to be prepared for the eventuality. If I do, I'll have to hire a full-time employee to look after the farm, and someone to keep Mum company. Naturally, I would be at home every weekend, as well as during the breaks. I would continue to oversee the farm and run it, but would need someone to take care of the day-to-day operations. The farm isn't so far from Reykjavik that it would be a major problem driving back east on the weekends. Then there are the long breaks between sessions, and I could always do committee work by computer. It would all work out. In many respects, it could be good to be away for a while, broaden my horizons and distance myself from everything in a certain sense. Ljótarstaðir would still be a sanctuary from the daily wrangling because my farm is so remote. There's no mobile phone connection in the farmhouse or the other buildings – which is another reason why my tractor cab out in the fields makes such a good office.

But this sanctuary at Ljótarstaðir depends on my not losing the land, on protecting it from the destructive effects of the Búland Power Plant. With massive building works just over the next hill, my privacy would be shot. The proposed construction is massive: canals here and levees there, up and down the entire area, all the way to Hólaskjól. But don't ask me to show you the maps; I can't bear to look at this monstrosity again.

It's so important to draw people's attention to this issue and to the bullying tactics of those who want to implement these plans. They think that they can stifle resistance simply by offering more money, and that any farmer or landowner will eventually give in. These power-plant thugs believe that they can get those opposed to them to stop with their nonsense – as in my case. I want to show others who are in the same boat that they don't have to give in. There are ways to resist. They could get involved politically. I want to tell people they have the right to be here and to stay here, and don't have to bow down to these bullies. So what if they have more money.

My farm gives me a different type of wealth, with a different potency. This land that I'm owner of today, which I have at my disposal for now, is an immense fortune. And I don't have to hand it over when a few big shots from Reykjavik come waving their money around.

Regarding going into parliament, it so happens that I once composed this rather un-rosy verse:

In parliament's halls their days to spend,
thinking that somehow the world they'll mend,
one or two go, and there they shout,
trying to bring a few changes about –
yet all of us know how Christ met his end.

If I don't get in, at least I've tried. I want to make a difference, to do something about the situation instead of just sitting at home and criticizing. It's unfair to hang around at home and pretend to have all the answers instead of trying to go and do things better. I've often criticized MPs and the government in the past. Now I have an opportunity to try my hand at it. It would be very much in the spirit of a person who sits at the kitchen table to have turned this opportunity down.

I've always been so involved in physical labour that it would be a huge challenge to take a sedentary job in parliament. But if I did happen to be elected, I would definitely be happy to return, after four years, to the good old grind.

21 AUGUST

The end of haymaking is at last in sight. It's all done at home, but we have yet to finish at Hvammur. The past few days, the weather hasn't been on our side, but the hay can lie there a little longer before it begins to pale. It helps that it's late summer and colder out, so it takes longer for it to go bad. Yesterday we mowed forty-three hectares. Just as well that it's not supposed to rain. Of course this is horribly stressful. A few years ago, I would have been certifiably insane if things were like this, but I'm becoming much calmer.

In this area, we talk about the hay 'paling', rather than 'yellowing', as they do almost everywhere else. If the hay starts paling and going bad, we talk about gathering the 'bleached'. And then we feed the animals 'the bleached'.

It's okay if part of the hay pales. You try to dry it out as much as possible. The animals will eat it, of course, but the quality is worse.

The faster the hay dries in the field the better. Every hour that the hay lies there, it loses more nutrients. But the weather has to be really dry for the hay not to have to lie there for a day and a half or so. It's warmest and driest at the end of June, when the days are longest. You get fewer good drying days as the summer progresses.

All the hay bales have been stacked at my farm. It's crucial to get them home as soon as possible. Bales are too valuable to ruin by letting them lie there in the field, and it's also bad for the fields. Each bale costs five to six thousand krónur to produce, and sells for about eight thousand.

25 AUGUST

Now the sheep have started to come home. They prefer being back in their home pastures once the vegetation starts to wither. Every year, some return before we head up to the heaths and slopes to round them up. You've got no choice but to open the gate to allow these early returnees onto the fenced pastures or lower hayfields, both for their own sake and the lambs', because they're quick to devour the grass outside the fence, and then they start losing weight. This weekend I'll round up the sheep in the fenced pastures and take the lambs from their mothers, before I head up to the highland pastures.

As it turns out, it's going to be a complicated job putting the new roofing on Rimma. The forecast isn't promising, and this type of project requires just the right weather. It can't rain, because the insulation is unprotected as we replace the corrugated iron sheets. It can't be windy either, because then everything just blows away.

Up here it rains a lot, which makes all work outdoors more difficult. But there's little else to do but put on your coveralls and tackle the work that can be done despite the rain.

29 AUGUST

I didn't feel the earthquakes that shook Katla last night, the strongest ones on record. I'm a bit scared, but there's no use thinking about it too much because then you end up thinking about nothing else. As my sheep are scattered all over the place, it would be really bad timing if Katla were to erupt now. It would be a bit better if it did so after I've got them all home and safe.

30 AUGUST

I'm so happy, and relieved; we've managed to get the new roof on the sheep-house Rimma. Siggeir and I worked on it together for the first two days. The weather was remarkable, absolutely calm. Otherwise, we wouldn't have been able to handle those big iron sheets – just the two of us – as it's impossible to do so in the wind. The weather was so fine and dry that we could leave all the rolls of roofing felt up there in the evening, and they were still there waiting for us like fine ladies the next morning.

On the final day, my friend Hjalti came to help us, along with Adda from Herjólfsstaðir. Adda brought Fífill's sister Rökkva with her. The two dogs had a blast – they goofed around and played the whole day. Fífill was naughty, though. He got hold of a chalk line reel that we were using to mark where the roof was to be nailed, and destroyed it. Then he found the coloured chalk that's put in the reel, chewed a hole in the container and turned his paws all red.

Unlike me, Siggeir is always calm. He said that it didn't matter, he had another container of chalk. I had another reel too, so it turned out all right. But it's guaranteed that you can't do anything here on the farm without an animal following what you're up to, whether it's a dog, a cat or a goat.

Next on the schedule is a meeting with the round-up committee about final preparations: to go over the lists of participants and see which groups need people. A cook has to be hired, a round-up boss, a corral manager. Before I set off for the highland pastures on 4 September, I need to take a day to run errands in Reykjavik and Selfoss. I need to buy some oil filters and oil for my quad bike, rubber shoes and some liquor for the crew at the home corral.

THE HOUSEHOLD
AT LJÓTARSTAÐIR

This feels like a good moment to go into more detail about my family and how it all works. My mum, Helga, is from Reykjavik, and has family roots in Öræfi, in south-east Iceland. She's the granddaughter of Bjarni from Vogur, who was a poet, an MP and a teacher of Greek and Latin. Her father was Bjarni Bjarnason, a lawyer for the office of the city magistrate. Mum's childhood home is one of those big, beautiful houses on Túngata, number 16. Now Haraldur Örn, her cousin, lives there.

So Mum was a city kid who fell in love with the countryside. For much of her childhood, she spent her summers at Hvarf in Bárðardalur, in northern Iceland. When she was in her third year of high school, she came here to Ljótarstaðir to work on a farm for the summer. Very soon afterwards, she married Sverrir, the son of the couple at the farm, who was living here with them. Mum and Sverrir had my sister Stella, and Ásta just over a year later. Then she went back and finished high school. She says that she owes that to her teacher Einar Magnússon, who later became rector. He happened to run into her in Reykjavik one day after she'd given up on her diploma, and he encouraged her to finish it.

Mum and Sverrir then had a third daughter, Arndís.

In 1967, when he was around thirty, Sverrir died in an avalanche in the mountains here west of Ljótarstaðir while searching for sheep in a bad storm. Mum mourned Sverrir deeply, and still keeps his memory sacred to this day. She was determined to keep his farm going, despite her three small girls and the difficulty of the land. Then Ásgeir, Sverrir's brother, quit his job as a sailor and moved here to help his brother's widow with the farm. One thing led to another and Dad and Mum had Fanney in 1971. I'm the youngest of the five daughters, born in 1978.

I got my name from Dad wanting me to be named Guðný, after his favourite aunt, but Mum wasn't content with me being named just Guðný, so she got to choose my second name. The big girls, as Fanney and I call our older sisters (just as they call us 'the little girls'), put in their two-pennies' worth, giving Mum an idea. Fanney had a big, beautiful picture book about Heidi, the girl who lived up in the Swiss Alps with her grandfather. The big girls wanted me to be named after her. Mum liked the idea – after all, our farm is a heath farm, which is *heiðarbýli* in Icelandic. So I was named Heiða Guðný. Dad was one of the few people who always called me by my full name. Everyone else calls me Heiða.

My family on my father's side comes from the Skaftafell district, and Dad and his siblings grew up in Álftaver. My Uncle Sverrir was highly skilled in versifying and wrote an ode to Skaftártunga that's sometimes called the anthem of the people of Tunga and starts with the words 'Skaftártunga, fair and bright'.

The brothers, Sverrir and Dad, were very different in appearance and personality, but both were masters of language. Dad was well-known for his wry humour. One of his descriptions of a person was this: 'a leading loser'. People round here still quote quite a few of his pithy one-liners.

Dad liked to joke around and was a great favourite with kids, particularly Linda and Ella from Úthlíð. He always took an interest in people and wanted to know how others were doing. He was always there for his friends if they wanted or needed to talk.

But most of the people on my father's side of the family are cold, and he could be cold too. One of the things that particularly characterized Dad was his very strong opinions and how he stuck to them. There were three things that he always insisted on when we were little. First, we had to eat breakfast. He would get terribly angry at the slightest chance of that not happening – if, for instance, we simply didn't want to. Second, we were supposed to wear hats, preferably all the time. And we weren't allowed to wear boots unless it was necessary. If we came outside wearing rubber boots in fine weather, he would forcibly pull them off us and hurl them aside. Because of this, I always eat breakfast and usually wear something on my head. I do, however, wear rubber footwear – not boots, but rubber shoes. Whether it's in reaction to Dad's three commandments or not, Mum doesn't eat breakfast, almost never wears a hat and likes wearing rubber boots.

Mum is cheerful. She's calm and is quick to laugh. My sisters have inherited these good qualities from her. I have my quirks and flaws, which I'm very well aware of and make real efforts to keep under control. There's my temper, for one thing. And it can be hard to get me to change my mind once I've made a decision about something.

It has long been the custom here on the farm to give everything names. When Stella was little, her cat was named 'Ketilbrandur, the Bishop's Foster Son'. Her dad, my Uncle Sverrir, gave it that name. I guess you could say that the brothers were pretty similar in this respect.

Dad's puns and witty expressions were endless. A light wooden-shafted hammer that I had was called 'Guðmundur, Bishop of Hólar' all its hammer life. Two good bottle lambs were named Straw Hat and Portly Tobbi. Common characters were, for example, Stóregont, who was mainly Dad himself, Studiosus and Hermundur Sky-pisser. Scarf and Engelred were dolls' names. It was contagious. My friend Linda and I commonly addressed each other as 'Thou royal plague rat'. Dad used honorifics all the time, for extra emphasis.

Naturally, we took part in all of this and gave our own names to everything and everyone, called Dad everything under the sun and sang him nonsense songs; there was always a lot of goofing around. Mum is a great comedian. She has a deep love of the Icelandic language and put special emphasis on teaching us correct spellings and ridding us of whatever grammatical errors we sisters made.

Starting shortly after she first arrived at the farm, Mum gave home-school lessons here at Ljótarstaðir, which suited her well. Like her, we five sisters have all done teaching of one kind or another, Fanney in particular.

Mum was more highly educated than is usual here in the countryside; she brought books and a zeal for learning with her. She often read out loud to us, and we got our interest in reading and deep respect for books from her. My all-time favourite moments have been winter evenings spent curled up with a book.

Dad was moved to the nursing home in Kirkjubæjarklaustur in 2006, when his cancer suddenly spread, attacking his entire body. When he also contracted pneumonia, Fanney and I stayed with him. At his worst, he couldn't sleep at night and was delirious at times, stuck in an endless sheep round-up. Fanney and I took turns keeping him company, herding over hill and dale with him, while whichever one of us wasn't herding tried to get some sleep on a mattress in the corner.

Once in the middle of the night, Dad suddenly felt as if nothing was going right and said to me, rather agitatedly: 'This isn't working! You've got to call out "ho," Heiða Guðný. Say "HO!" Say "ho ho!"'

In the corner, Fanney looked frazzled – how would this end? You can't be shouting 'ho' in the middle of the night in a nursing home. But I had a flash of inspiration and said to him: 'We'd better keep quiet, now, Dad. The sheep are starting to go through the gate.' That worked, for a time. But it wouldn't have done any good to shush him; that would have been like trying to shush the north wind.

No matter how confused he was, he never got Fanney and me mixed up. He'd ask her: 'Where's Heiða Guðný?' 'She's blocking the way,' Fanney replied.

He'd ask me: 'Why isn't Fanney coming?' I had to think of something, and replied: 'Because you sent her up the river.'

Various nonsensical things happened in the midst of Dad's long round-up. Sudden demands: 'Give me more coffee, Oddbjörg.' Apparently, his sister had shown up with the coffeepot, just like that, in the middle of it all.

The nurses were unsurprised. It's common for old farmers in nursing homes to believe that they're still doing farm work. Another farmer there was constantly moving chairs around – in other words, either driving the cows home or letting them out of the barn.

Once Dad had recovered from his pneumonia, I asked him if he wanted to come home. He said that he did, and Mum and I nursed him here at the farm through his two remaining months. Fanney came and brought María with her every weekend and at Christmas to help us look after him, and my sister Ásta also stopped in frequently during this time.

The nurse came once a week. Our doctor helped us a lot, as well, and even stopped by without us asking.

We didn't have any other professional help. Dad was very brave. Of course he was frightened, too; he knew what was coming.

I had to resort to all kinds of techniques while nursing Dad – a task that wasn't made any easier by how big and heavy he still was. When I had to get him up and dressed in the mornings, I had no other choice but to yank him into a sitting position. Every time I jolted him, he would just huff, until one day he finally protested: 'Aw, Heiða Guðný, I'm always a little worried that you'll rip my elbow off its mainland.'

Dad is buried here at Gröf in Skaftártunga. There he rests next to his parents, his brother and my sister Arndís. My old Lux, the white Toyota pick-up truck, is a gift from him. Apart from that, he never gave me anything. The Lux has held up well. Built in 2000, it has been driven 380,000 kilometres.

Mum and Dad always stuck to their roles, with Dad as the farm manager and Mum as the widow who owned the business. They never considered themselves a couple, despite living together. The word 'family' was never used. Mum was determined that we would always be the 'household', never the 'family', at Ljótarstaðir. My parents kept all of their possessions and finances separate, and made no secret of it. This policy of separation went so far that visitors came either to see Dad or Mum, never both together.

Of course, this was considered strange, something that I was often aware of. Why they behaved like this, I don't know, and it's not for me to guess. This much is certain: it wasn't out of necessity. Both of them had had all kinds of other opportunities, those elegant people. Dad was a particularly handsome man and Mum is gorgeous.

I think that Mum and Dad had happy years here together at the start. My sisters remember good times. But then their arrangement soured, and for a period, they didn't even speak to each other. Dad was so down about it that he wouldn't talk to us girls for days at a time. But this darkness is something that derives from human pain, not malice . . . I see that now.

The first time I had to put down a sheep happened because of a lack of communication with Dad. The sheep was very sick and something had to be done in the situation, but Dad wouldn't answer me. So, seeing that he'd already taught me how to use the gun, I just went and did the deed. A farmer has to be able to put down animals. Doing so, however, has always been hard for me, and it hasn't got any easier over the years.

My three older sisters, Sverrir's daughters, always called my dad Ásgeir. When talking about him, they called him 'foster father'.

For several years after Arndís died and Stella and Ásta had left home, Fanney and I were the only children on the farm. It all happened so quickly. We were here, all five of us sisters, then all of a sudden the three oldest ones were gone. Stella and Ásta left home around the same time, and when Arndís got hurt she never came home again.

The plan had always been for Arndís to take over the farm. I think that Dad lost much of his spark after she died. He was fatigued; he'd taken on the farm operations and three little girls, who then became five. Then he was back at the beginning, raising a three-year-old and a ten-year-old.

Dad didn't particularly push us to attend school after the age of sixteen, but he really didn't want me, or Fanney, to take over the farm. He only came back to help after his brother died so suddenly, and he always found the isolation of Ljótarstaðir difficult. Dad struggled with the darkness of winter. And then Arndís's death hit him really hard and the valleys grew deeper and the peaks lower.

My sisters and I are all close, but my relationship with Fanney is particularly special because she took care of me when Mum was in Reykjavik with Arndís. I think Fanney probably still feels responsible for me. When she left home to continue her schooling, I was aged nine and the only kid left at Ljótarstaðir. There was always a bunch of other kids here during the summers, though. When all of my sisters were still at home, there were usually upwards of ten of us. We played a lot in Bæjargil Ravine and at that wonderful place on the river where the farm creek flows into it, abiding by our parents' strict rules in order to avoid danger.

We got to camp out in the ravine to the east of the farm, and the older kids slept out in the tent most of the summer. The bright summers of my childhood, spent out in nature here at home in Ljótarstaðir, are memories I always carry with me, close at hand.

We all wrote eulogies for Dad after he died. Fanney and I wrote this one together:

> Dearest Dad, there are so many things that spring to mind when we think about you. Top of the list, though, is that no matter what you were up to, we were always there with you. We weren't very big when you woke us up in the morning, waited while we ate breakfast and then led us by the hand or pulled us on the toboggan to the sheep-houses at the top of the field.
>
> We always firmly believed that all of this was because it was important to you to have us with you, even though recently we've begun to suspect that we may have been in the way more than anything else. But this taught us the lesson you always emphasized, that everyone should help out with the daily work, and everyone should be given a task suited to their age and development.
>
> It couldn't have escaped anyone's notice when you were out and about with your girls. We were forever teasing each other, both verbally and physically, and you didn't always come out on top. We remember the scuffles over your hat, buckets tied together, flying hay bales and races in which every trick in the book was used. You

also taught us many good verses too – some that Mum wasn't allowed to hear – and clever stories about our ancestors – 'the old folks,' as you called them – and we particularly loved breaking the snow ceilings off the creek together.

Thank you for all our years together, and for being there for us through good times and bad. We will spend many happy times in the years to come recalling the things you said and reminiscing about various characters from the past. We miss you.

Fanney and Heiða Guðný

ARNDÍS

My sister Arndís died when she was seventeen. In July 1981, she fell while climbing the cliffs of the Hjörleifshöfði inselberg mountain. She was in hospital in Reykjavik for around six months after the accident, and died in late January 1982. I was three years old at the time.

This is what led to the accident: when Arndís had got to the top of the cliffs with her friends, she took off her scarf and threw it down. After they'd descended, however, she realized that the scarf had got stuck halfway down and decided to climb up after it, athlete that she was. She probably didn't like the prospect of heading back down from the place where she retrieved the scarf, so she climbed up higher. But just as she got to the top the edge crumbled, and she fell dozens of metres all the way down.

The accident left her paralysed and unable to communicate, but she seemed to be aware of others. There was never any hope of recovery, I think; it was just a matter of time before she died. She died of pneumonia, as is common in such circumstances.

Mum was in Reykjavik with Arndís; Dad stayed at home with me, the farmhand Árni and Fanney, who was then ten years old. My sister Stella came by every now and then, as did Ásta; they had both already left home by the time this happened. Ásta was at Ásar in Skaftártunga, and Stella was in Reykjavik.

They all managed as well as they could. Dad was used to looking after himself; the young Árni was tough as nails, and Fanney was an extremely bright and industrious child. In the absence of Mum, Dad taught her how to make rice porridge and boil haddock and to put together shopping lists for us all.

Mum stayed with her family in Reykjavik until the autumn, and she and Stella were at the hospital most of the time. During those months, Fanney and I were caught in a kind of limbo. The situation wasn't really ever discussed. The only thing said was: Mum will come home as soon as Arndís is better.

At that time, grief counselling was unheard of, so nothing of the sort was available to Mum when Arndís died, nor for her earlier loss of Sverrir.

I went to the hospital once to visit Arndís after she got injured. That visit is burned into my brain, and is still among the most painful memories found there. For years afterwards, I suffered something like panic attacks if I had to go anywhere near a hospital. It was enough just to catch a whiff of one.

It was easier for me than for the others, though. At that age, children are mainly preoccupied with themselves; they can't help it. I can't begin to imagine what the rest of my family went through.

*   *   *

Arndís was always kind to me and played with me a lot. Even though I was so young when she died, my limited memories of her are very precious to me. I remember a visit to the National Hospital when she had an operation for a slipped disc in her back, a year before the accident. The nurse took me to get an orange, which Arndís and I then ate, sitting on her hospital bed.

One of my clearest memories is of her coming home after getting her driver's licence. Dad went and got her, and I waited excitedly in the window to see her driving. But it was just Dad who drove back. I ran and asked Arndís why she hadn't driven, and she said she didn't drive old junkers like her foster father's Gaz 69. I felt highly insulted on Dad's behalf, but he just grinned.

I also clearly remember my third birthday, and Arndís being at my birthday party. Few things are dearer to me than the card with the special poem that Arndís gave me then:

Coffee and cake are finally here,
which makes me so happy, and how!
Heiða's now starting her number-four year . . .
Hurrah to our wonderful, big girl now!

AUTUMN

New energy comes to all in the spring
and then throughout summer birds merrily sing.
But next comes damned autumn,
and what does work bring
besides runny noses? Hardly a thing.

POWER OF THE SEASONS

Ever since I was a child, I've had a strong sense of the power of nature and its contrasts. In the summer, nature and my mountains feel like a nursery. The lambs go to the mountains as little fluff balls and return practically full-grown. Many birds nest here on my land, as the place names indicate: Gæsár (Goose River) and Gæsárdalir (Goose River Valleys). Then there's Gæsatungur (Goose Promontories), which is a huge stretch of land along the Tungufljót River, where both the pink-footed goose and greylag goose nest. These would be among the areas flooded by the reservoir for the Búland Power Plant.

So much goes on in the summer out in gentle nature, which gives life to all, birds and beasts. And it's fun for people who are physically capable to spend as much of the summertime as they can in the wilderness.

Recently, I've been leading hikes for the purpose of acquainting visitors with the grandeur of the Icelandic wilderness. I take groups on an approximately three-hour hike from Ljótarstaðir to Sýrdalur, an area of incomparable beauty that hardly anyone knows about.

Along the way are gems of nature such as Hrossafoss (Horse Falls), with its robust-sounding name. The hike's main focus is on the area along the Tungufljót River and the gorges, those unique constructions of nature. For me, it's wonderful to lift the veil from my countryside, reveal it and tell others about it.

Once autumn arrives, nature finally demonstrates its deadly power. The birds flee for warmer climes and, no matter what, the sheep have to be brought home. Now they're in great peril in exactly the same place where they've enjoyed such blissful summer days – in bright nature, which has the awesome power to nourish these animals, allow them to grow and thrive, gently and generously.

In wintertime, the whole environment becomes harsh and dangerous. It's completely different to travel in the summer versus the winter. Up in the heath pastures in the summer, the days are endless; the rivers gurgle and everything is beautiful. When I'm in the wild on my snowmobile in wintertime, the days are short, the cold piercing and the familiar landscape so transformed that I have a hard time accustoming myself to all its alterations. If the forecast is fair, everything is safe, but as soon as a storm blows in it's perilous to be in the wilderness areas around and beyond my farm.

But even in winter, that dangerous season, the beauty of the mountains can be overwhelming. And autumn is a chapter of its own. On autumn days and mornings, the air is crystal clear and free of mist. That's when we do the secondary round-ups. Sometimes the mountains have just begun to whiten. That's fine – because then even the most diehard sheep come down. This is the best time to be out in the mountains, surrounded by autumnal colours and vast spreading views.

THE FIGHT OVER THE
BÚLAND POWER PLANT

In 2010, the CEO of the Suðurorka energy company came out here to Skaftártunga for the first time, to explore possibilities for the development and construction of the Búland Power Plant. He also came here to Ljótarstaðir. He was a pen-pusher from Reykjavik with slicked-back hair and spotless hands.

He came to the stable, acting terribly smarmy, and hung around for two hours with me and my then boyfriend. He talked and talked and said that he was interested in buying a colt of ours called The Son of Smári; and then he and my boyfriend went for a test ride. There were geese pecking at the grass on the home hayfield. A few times a day, I would send Adda's German Shepherd bitch out to drive them away, to keep them from damaging the field. I'd just sent her on that same mission, but called her back, remembering how touchy The Son of Smári could be. The geese could have scared him right up onto the heath if they'd flown up screeching right by the road. I didn't need to worry about my boyfriend: he was the kind of horseman who could ride any horse, and never fall off. But I knew nothing about the other rider and didn't want to be frightening his horse out from under him. Ever since then and during this fight, though, I've often regretted losing such a great opportunity there to witness this particular visitor fall off his horse.

After that, the Suðurorka man kept showing up here in the countryside. He even came two autumns and herded sheep with us on the last day of the round-ups. The rest of us herders were pretty surprised to see him, but didn't let it bother us. He was also at the corral for sorting, and showed up at the round-up dance.

Suðurorka is a company that I've never really understood. I don't know who exactly owns it, but one thing is certain: it must be sitting on a lot of capital, because this has been going on since at least 2010. And Suðurorka has only one project on its agenda: the Búland Power Plant. When the National Power Company of Iceland gave up on the development of a power plant here, it sold its existing data on the project to Suðurorka. It's a huge construction project that extends to the boundary of our national park, the Highland Centre at Hólaskjól, which attracts numerous tourists, down through Skaftártunga, all the way south to the Ring Road near Hrífunes in the east and Ásar in the west – with a little stop at Ljótarstaðir – and a ten-square-kilometre reservoir in my canyon, Rásgljúfur, right on my main pastureland, with a corresponding monster of a dam!

It was some time before I began taking these plans seriously. I simply couldn't believe that this absurdity would ever become a reality. But the same could be said about many who'd been confronted by the Kárahnjúkar Power Plant – among them a man who came from Egilsstaðir to our public meeting in Tungusel in 2014 to show us photos of that monstrosity back east. He said that he hadn't put up a strong enough resistance because he hadn't believed it would actually be built. And I didn't believe it either, despite the Búland Power Plant already being included in the master plan. I was hardly alone in my disbelief. The project rapidly became a running joke in this area. When we were rounding up the sheep, we'd say: 'Just think, we'll be doing this on speedboats next time.' But I've been kicking myself every day since for having allowed this beast to slip into the master plan.

I only woke up to the seriousness of the situation when good friends of mine demanded: 'Are you *really* going to let this happen to you?' And then I suddenly saw that this power plant could indeed become a reality – in which case, I would be forced to defend myself. But I consider myself a peaceful person and it isn't really in my nature to fight.

The struggle began for real in 2012, when we had to argue against the sitting municipal council, whose members were highly supportive of ideas for power-harnessing projects in Skaftártunga. In the summer of 2012, two men came to Ljótarstaðir to discuss the plans for the Búland Power Plant with me. I received these men politely, and even gave them coffee, but I made my position completely clear. Nevertheless, they tried calling me later to let me know that some studies were going to be conducted. I told them again that I didn't want this power plant on my land; and that none of it would ever be for sale. I'd made this same statement repeatedly since 2010. I hung up on them and they didn't call again. It was in that year, 2012, that I began writing articles for newspapers and speaking at various meetings. I finally felt forced to take action.

When the man from Suðurorka became more and more unpopular here in our district, he was quietly replaced with another, whom we shall call the Negotiator. He's a charming, clever fellow, a former farmer from Ingjaldssandur. What's more, he speaks the same language as the rest of us farmers. From what I understand, he'd previously been working on making deals for smaller power-plant projects with landowners elsewhere.

In January 2012, the Negotiator invited four people from Skaftártunga who had publicly expressed their opposition to meet him at the Tungusel Community Centre and discuss the matter. There, he convinced us of the usefulness of establishing an advisory committee that would deal with the impact assessment report for the Búland Power Plant. Such a report already existed but hadn't yet been published. The advisory committee would serve the purpose of providing all stakeholders with a vehicle through which they could voice their opinions, better equipping them to file oppositions during the consultation process.

He specifically emphasized to us the importance of finding a viable way to assess the different impact factors, including social impact. For example, the value of the existence of family seats, where people could go home to their own farms – the farms where they had roots of some sort. There was also talk about a viable assessment of the value of the Tungufljót River. And whether it was possible to assess emotional impact. Perhaps it simply wasn't possible to find viable ways to assess all of these things. Perhaps these values were incalculable. In which case, of course, there would be no power plant.

We were also told that dividend payments would be made to all the affected farms. That was new – that there would be dividends from the power plant for fifty to sixty years, tied to farms, not people.

I was polite at this meeting, even if it was clear where I stood. The Negotiator said that he could persuade the Suðurorka people to share the environmental impact assessment report with the four of us, provided that we handle it responsibly. We agreed, and each of us was given a copy. In other words, I agreed to be one of those allowed to view the report. We were handed our copies of this tome only after signing a confidentiality agreement stating that we would never publicly disclose anything written in it. We then had to sign a contract verifying this, and our names were stamped on every page of our respective copies.

At two meetings that the four of us had with the Negotiator, he hinted at impending changes to the Watercourses Act; that is, if more than one party owned the rights to a certain body of water, then another party (for instance, the landowner on the opposite side of the river) would no longer have a say over the land on their side. According to the current laws, people have authority over their own side of the river or stream, and from the bank out into the middle of it. They don't have to go along with it if the landowner on the other side wants to permit the construction of a reservoir. The new laws, however, would have changed all that. In my case, it would have meant that I couldn't block a reservoir being constructed in my pastureland if the landowner on the other side of the river wanted to sell his land for it. These alleged impending changes to the law have yet to be implemented. Much later, I discussed this with lawyers who specialize in such matters, and they said that they were unaware of any such proposed changes to the law. Let alone that they'd gone into effect.

In retrospect, it seems quite clear that I was invited to the meetings at Tungusel only so that afterwards it could be claimed to those working on the master plan that I'd been involved as a member of the advisory committee. But I was never on such a committee. On the other hand, I fell for this trick. I thought that it might be good for morale if we could all have a look at the environmental impact assessment report, thus giving everyone a better chance to form their own opinions of it. And that we would then unite to defend ourselves when the time came. Don't forget, I'm a sheep farmer and am not versed in legal niceties.

A good example of how the power-plant people go about their work is when, at the Tungusel meetings, the Negotiator stated that no one had ever before managed to stop the construction of a power plant in Iceland. Of course this isn't true. For example, Sigríður from Brattholt successfully fought to protect the waterfall Gullfoss. The Eyjabakkar wetlands, one of the world's main breeding grounds for the pink-footed goose, were also successfully protected from the encroachment of the Fljótsdalur Power Plant project following a public outcry.

At our first meeting at Tungusel, the Negotiator spoke as if he was on our side. He declared that an environmental advisory committee was necessary to ensure that all points of view would have a chance to be expressed and that the people in this area would be better equipped to file oppositions when the public notice process began. This – and only this – was what we were led to believe.

Then we began discussing the best forum for all the residents of Skaftártunga. There is currently just one association: the Angling Association of Skaftártunga. Two of the four who attended the Tungusel meetings were also on its board. So they called for an association meeting.

All the farms in Skaftártunga belong to the Angling Association, and the first meeting was well attended. The Negotiator presented his proposal for an advisory committee for the environmental impact assessment report, and four people were elected to it: two who were already opposed to the power plant, one in favour of it and, finally, the resident at Búland. The Negotiator suggested Ella and me, knowing we were just about to start pregnancy scanning and would be away for the next six weeks. The Negotiator offered to work with the advisory committee at the start. But he could be excluded at any time.

While Ella and I were away, the municipal council received a letter the Negotiator had written on behalf of an advisory committee formed by the Angling Association, in which a request was made for an option on an abandoned farm owned by the municipality and located to the east of the Skaftá River. The option was described as compensation for the pastureland that the farmers of Skaftártunga would lose to the Búland Power Plant. The letter was forwarded to the round-up committees, of which there are four. The response of the committees was muted – so much so that I don't know if the letter was ever answered or not.

So here it looked as if the advisory committee that had been set up to keep its eye on the environmental impact assessment had started trying to come up with solutions, to make proposals for compensatory measures and, among other things, to involve itself in the master plan of Skaftá Municipality.

A menacing silence fell over Skaftártunga. From that time on, it felt as if those who were opposed to the power plant had little to say to me. The municipal council elections were coming up. Various conservationist types and those opposed to power plants both here in this district and elsewhere pushed for me to stand for office in a new political party that put environmental issues and conservation to the fore. Due to my time pressures, I wasn't keen. And I've never had any desire to be in the spotlight; quite the opposite.

I ended up taking the first position on the ballot for this party, despite not having a minute to spare. The result was that they got one person elected to the municipal council: me. The election resulted in no majority, so instead it was decided that a coalition would be formed, and a formal agreement concluded, after all parties made compromises. We had to back down on our demanded revision of the master plan, but it was agreed that all discussion of power-plant construction would be tabled for that term. If the council had to choose a position, for instance regarding the consultation process for the master plan, then that position would always be neutral. This was of course far from what I would have wanted, but was a great victory in light of the ongoing agenda.

At the start of 2015, this coalition fell apart and I became the vice-chairman of Skaftá Municipality. I would never have gone into local government had I not had to defend myself, and not just myself, but my district, my land and the entire country, in fact. I've really struggled with being in politics, not just because I have so little free time, but also because I find it so difficult to speak in public. Added to which, I don't like meetings and my job on the council means loads of those – on top of the ones that I already attend as a committee member for Vatnajökull National Park. This also means a lot of time lost from my farm work in travelling to these meetings.

On 1 May 2014, the Icelandic Environment Association and Eldvötn, a local environmental conservation group, held a public meeting on power plants and power harnessing at Tungusel. At the time, it was a struggle to get people to talk about power plants, so once more they invited me. The original plan had been to invite someone else, but no one was interested. Very few people from Skaftártunga showed up, and none of them were vocal opponents of the Búland Power Plant. At the end of August the Angling Association decided to hold a meeting on the advisory committee's work. I was invited to the meeting with less than a day's notice, and was already booked in at other meetings. The advisory committee had been downsized and an attempt had been made to bring in people from the municipal council. But the council refused to become involved, stating that any involvement on its part would have to be unbiased.

At the time, a coalition of all the different parties still existed. At the meeting, plans were introduced for the establishment of a Development Fund for Skaftártunga, which would work to secure dividend payments from the power-plant operation for all the farms in Skaftártunga. But Suðurorka had been planning to withhold most of this money, according to an amendment made to previously-concluded agreements with the people who owned the water rights to the Skaftá River. The first payments according to those agreements were supposed to have been made that summer, but they were not

At the end of September 2015, the Angling Association held an informational meeting at Tungusel. I couldn't attend because I was busy with a meeting organized by the Icelandic Environment Association in Reykjavik, but I got the chairman of the Angling Association to read and distribute a presentation that I'd given at a meeting at Tungusel that same autumn. At the Angling Association's meeting, the advisory committee resigned, and the meeting voted to entrust their board with the task of carrying out the committee's work. The board of the Angling Association continued to meet with the Suðurorka man, who was asked to read, among other things, a draft water rights agreement, draft proposals for the apportionment of the dividend payments made by the power plant, as outlined in registered letters, and a draft contract made between Suðurorka and the landowners and water rights holders. There are only three farms in the construction area of the Búland Power Plant, and Ljótarstaðir is one of them. But it is vital because it holds water rights to both Skaftá and Tungufljót.

Around the end of November, I received a registered letter outlining the work of the advisory committee and the proposals for the apportionment of the dividends from the power plant between landowners and water rights holders. I found it very hard to read as I had always made it clear that I would never sell my water rights, but I forced myself to glance through it. Then an email inviting me to a meeting at a specific time with the Suðurorka man arrived in my inbox at half past ten in the evening. He wanted to meet with us all separately. I immediately sent him a very strongly worded reply, saying that if he and his company continued to apply such coercive methods, I would raise one hell of a storm. I let him know that there were others besides Suðurorka who could play fast and loose with threats. Writing it cost me a sleepless night, and my pulse was racing. In these kinds of circumstances, I feel as if a knife has been thrust between my ribs – almost as if I'm having a heart attack. Even now, just thinking about it, I get a stabbing pain in my chest and my shoulder muscles tense.

Nor did it help, dealing with these awful situations there in the winter darkness, that I was alone on the farm. Mum had been in the hospital since November with a bad infection in her knee and an uncertain prognosis.

I didn't attend the meeting with the Suðurorka man. Why should I?

Another registered letter came. It contained the information that Suðurorka wanted to present to me at the meeting, laying out Ljótarstaðir's share of the dividend payments from the power plant for a number of years. I took a peek at it, but didn't read the letter all the way through. I started feeling anxious again. I had no idea where my neighbours stood. And I was afraid to call them to find out.

At that point, I consulted the Icelandic Environment Association, who said that I was going to need a lawyer. Once one of their lawyers had reviewed the situation, they recommended Ásgerður Ragnarsdóttir from the law firm Lex, who is a specialist in this field.

I'd felt like a voice crying in the wilderness. The Suðurorka men wouldn't listen and wouldn't understand, even after I'd told them over and over that we would never strike a deal. Once, one of them said: 'I'll just keep coming back again and again.' I replied: 'Be my guest.' His answer was: 'But you can be sure that I am not going to have to come forever.' It was a veiled threat.

I imagined that they would understand better if a lawyer became involved. From then on, she would deal with the letters sent to me and handle all other communications with Suðurorka. This was also good news for my postman, who had started running away as soon as he handed me registered letters. The moment I saw they were from Suðurorka, I would begin boiling like a steam kettle and come close to blowing my top.

Ásgerður sent a letter to Suðurorka, reiterating my position. I must admit, however, that I felt as if the onslaught of registered letters from Suðurorka smelled like a precursor to expropriation, so I was still worried. But my lawyer assured me that Suðurorka had no grounds to force my hand and all this was just empty threats.

It's a big step for a countrywoman like me to hire a lawyer. A bill for seventy thousand krónur (which, of course, I got) is a lot of money for a sheep farmer – enough to cover feed enhancer for my entire flock during lambing.

I'm not sure I would have dared to hire a lawyer if the environmental conservation associations hadn't pledged to back me financially. Luckily it didn't come to that; I ended up paying my bill, but if the amount had been any higher I would have had to avail myself of their support. The conservation associations have involved themselves before in cases like mine. Their support is absolutely essential, because this is how the energy industry gets people to bend – through money.

Right around the time that I hired a lawyer, in January 2016, the community dialogue was picking up speed and my neighbours' positions were becoming clearer. My nerves, however, had become so strained by the aggression of the Suðurorka men, the difficult meetings and divisiveness in the community, that I didn't even feel up to playing on my snowmobile any more. I felt so drained of *joie de vivre*, added to the pressing need to find the money to pay my lawyer's bills, that I mainly thought about selling it. On this farm, there's never any cash to spare. But somehow, I muddle through.

THE FIELD TRIP

At the beginning of the summer of 2015, I received an email about a proposed field trip for all the expert committees for the third phase of the master plan to the construction sites of the Hólmsá and Búland Power Plants. The municipal councils were asked to participate. The trip was scheduled for 5 September. I then had over three months to worry about it.

On Wednesday, 2 September, I was raking for my neighbours when I received an email reminder about the field trip in three days' time, asking who would be attending on behalf of the municipal council. An agenda was attached. There I saw that Suðurorka would be holding a presentation of their plans, complete with coffee and other refreshments, at the Tungusel Community Centre. But I wouldn't have heard about the meeting at all had I not been on the municipal council.

There were only forty-eight hours to go before the trip. In a rage, I grabbed my smartphone there in the tractor, while still raking, and immediately sent an email asking why Suðurorka was giving a presentation and not the National Power Company, which was in charge of the Hólmsá Power Plant project. I received a polite reply saying that Suðurorka's presentation would be indoors, while the National Power Company would be giving one outdoors.

In my naivety, I'd thought that the only ones attending would be the expert committees and municipal councils. Now that I realized what was going on, I started sending emails to everyone I could, asking whether, as a landowner, I could give a presentation as well. And I sent an email to our municipal council, asking whether I could act as a council member with regard to the Hólmsá Power Plant, and as a landowner with regard to the Búland Power Plant. And whether Jóna Björk, my deputy, could take over from me as a council member when it came to matters connected with Búland, allowing me to attend their presentation solely as a stakeholder.

By that point, my phone was white hot. I was so wound up that I forgot to lower the hay rake, leaving it hanging there spinning for an entire round. I did a piss-poor job raking that particular field. But to be honest, I was lucky not to wrap the whole contraption around the electricity poles. When I finally finished raking late that evening, I raced home to Ljótarstaðir, driving the tractor straight through the potholes.

My emails received a very good response; they agreed to all my requests. I promptly began composing my presentation in my head, while still thinking hard about the other things that I needed to do. I spent Thursday writing it. I needed to find photos taken with my hiking groups, photos from the area around Tungufljót. Then Fanney read over the presentation and threw it back in my face, telling me I had to tone it down. But by Friday, everything was more or less ready to go.

It started with the field trip the following day, Saturday. We took a look at some of the areas that would be affected by the Hólmsá Power Plant, including the site of the planned reservoir. A representative of the National Power Company made a presentation. On the bus with the expert committees, the members of the municipal council were given the opportunity to discuss the municipality's policies and the history of power-harnessing ideas for the area. This helped because I'm just as strongly opposed to the Hólmsá Power Plant. It's the same thing as Búland: the same madness, the same sort of area. In its entirety, this region is much more valuable as it is now than it would be with those power plants. The Búland Power Plant is an even more insane construction project. It's so overwhelming and unthinkable, in every aspect. To even imagine trying to control that monster, the Skaftá River, which itself is the very picture of arrogant ignorance!

Added to which, there are forty hectares of uncultivated woods in Skaftártunga, which have existed there since the first human settlers came to Iceland in the ninth century. These woods, called Villingaskógar, would all disappear beneath the proposed Hólmsá Reservoir. The National Power Company proposed planting eighty hectares of woods in their place, but they could never replace these last remnants of the most ancient Icelandic woodland.

A shining example of the backwardness of conservationism in Iceland is that when the Hólmsá Power Plant was first outlined in the master plan, these woods weren't even taken into account. It wasn't until Vigfús began leading hikes in the area that people finally became aware of the 'Settlement Woods,' and the waterfall in the Skógá River, which runs through them. Only then did people's minds begin to change.

The field trip continued, and at Tungusel we were offered the refreshments provided by Suðurorka. Jóna Björk showed up and took over my role of municipal council member, while I became a landowner, with my and Fanney's presentation all ready to go.

Among the attendees were all the Suðurorka upstarts, who had set up a flashy exhibition with all sorts of glossy photos. They referred emphatically to the work of the Skaftártunga Angling Association and the prevailing unity of the local community. The Suðurorka man made a big deal about the work done here in the community and the equitable apportionment of the dividends and, once again, the unity of the local community. It was outrageous. Such incredible arrogance! I was nauseated by their bullshit.

When it was my turn to speak, I criticized the way in which the developers had been given direct access to the municipal councils and expert committees, whereas no other stakeholders had been invited on this field trip. I made it clear that I was appalled that the developers got unrestricted access to the expert committees for the master plan and to the municipal councils, while the landowners did not. Then I gave my presentation, in which I directly refuted most of the things that the Suðurorka man had stated – including the creation of the so-called advisory committee and the status of supposed agreements.

It was now crystal clear to both Jóna Björk and me how important my election to the municipal council had been. Had I not been on the council, I would have had no idea that a field trip had been organized. If I hadn't been at that meeting at Tungusel, the Suðurorka men might have carried the day. They'd wanted to persuade their audience that the people in this community were unified in their support for the Búland Power Plant, and that their agreements with the holders of water rights to the Skaftá River were valid. I disputed this, despite not being one hundred per cent certain, and said that these agreements had been nullified by Suðurorka's failure to deliver on payments . . . that they actually hadn't paid a thing. It turned out that the Suðurorka man was unable to disprove this, which, of course, he would have done if I'd been wrong.

When I finished my talk, the room was deadly silent.

Then the Suðurorka man broke the silence, saying smoothly: 'It's always so fun to listen to Heiða. She's so articulate. And this time, she wasn't so far from the truth.'

They're such games-players, those bastards. They don't even have the guts to speak badly of you to your face!

But behind your back is another thing altogether. I later heard from others that the power-plant men said they didn't believe that the woman at Ljótarstaðir could run the farm on her own much longer. They made comments such as: 'She's always on her own. Of course, she'll eventually find a husband and move away.' I also heard about the exorbitant sums that they were apparently going to offer me for my land.

Following the meeting at Tungusel, the field trip continued on to the proposed site of the Búland Power Plant. It was huge. In addition to the ten-square-kilometre reservoir, loads of levees, irrigation ditches and water-use facilities would be needed.

I went to look because I was compelled to do so. I can't bear to see it all outlined on maps – all those transmission lines, canals and concrete walls, all that destruction, in my district, on my land. The proposed dam in Rásgljúfur Canyon would be nearly as tall as the tower of Hallgrímskirkja Cathedral. Imagine if that dam broke.

One of the things I pointed out was that if dammed, only a third of the volume of our Tungufljót River would flow past Ljótarstaðir. The Suðurorka men considered this nonsense. But I pointed out that the current at Ljótarstaðir wasn't the same as that at the current meter. Then I rattled off the names of all the streams and creeks that feed Tungufljót between the dam and Ljótarstaðir, and then all those that feed the river from Ljótarstaðir down to the current meter. It isn't easy fighting against a landowner who knows her entire area like the back of her hand.

*   *   *

In January 2016 came the news that the board of the Angling Association of Skaftártunga had ended its collaboration with Suðurorka. My lawyer told me that the activities of angling associations were clearly regulated by law and that they certainly did not involve negotiating with landowners over power-plant construction.

In retrospect, what happened was something like this: Suðurorka had manipulated the Angling Association for its own purposes, and gone on to it about the unified support for the power-plant project – and about how the Angling Association had put in such a great, selfless effort, especially regarding the advisory committee for the environmental impact assessment report.

And as the days began lengthening, I started feeling better – helped, of course, by the Angling Association ending its collaboration with the power plant and my having hired a lawyer. I also heard that few people here, if any, were satisfied with the draft agreements that Suðurorka had sent them. I felt much more relaxed heading off to do pregnancy scanning in February. And Mum was finally well enough to come home at last, after spending three months in hospital.

HEIÐA AT A POETRY MEET-UP

The Pots and Pans Revolution of 2009

When the organized protests over the financial crisis began in Reykjavik, I was seriously bummed out that we stopped doing our own butchering at Ljótarstaðir a long time ago. You see, I wouldn't have minded joining in those protests against the sitting government. One of the few things that old Dad and I agreed on was the need to stick a sharp horn deep in the side of the Progressive Party, and it would have been so appropriate to have shown up at those protests with some half-digested grass from a sheep's gut to throw. One thing the stuff has over paint and other such material is that it's completely organic, and would have just washed off the Alþingi Building in the next rain.

> Our country is sunk; it's been bested.
> Its parliament's halls – rat-infested.
> Before it let's gather,
> bang pots, shout, and slather
> its walls with sheep's food, fresh digested.

CATS AND DOGS
AT LJÓTARSTAÐIR

When I was little, the cats lived in the barn. But as they grew older, they began coming into the house and would lounge around the living room instead. I got a kitten the autumn I started ninth grade, and I adored her. She was my first housecat, named Loppa (Paw), but we always just called her Kisa (Kitty). She died in 2012, at a great age for a cat – almost twenty years old. So I had the same pet from the time that I was a teenager until well after becoming a farmer. The one flaw that my cat had was that she snored.

One of the indelible memories I have of my darling kitty was of her depositing mice and birds on my pillow the one time as an adult that I lay sick in bed for days. Normally, she never did that. When the doctor came to look in on me, Kisa hissed and looked as if she was going to attack him, so Mum had to lock her in another room during his visit.

She was cuddled up with me in bed when she died. I was so sad that I swore never to get another cat so that I wouldn't have to experience such grief again. But by noon the next day, I have to admit I already had my eye on another. I buried my old kitty beneath the trees in the garden. And I got a new cat.

Her name is Huggun (Solace), but I also call her Kisa for short. She was the cutest kitten, and tremendously fun to play with. But she also demands a lot of attention. And she has the odd habit of gently poking at my eyelids with her paw to wake me up. If that doesn't get my attention, she'll poke at my nose instead.

This cat is a fanatical hunter, so much so that she wears two bells. If you notice a tiny spot of blood on the floor of the shower in the morning, you know what's gone on there. She doesn't even leave the claws or tail of the mouse, as my old cat did. I don't understand how she does it. She must slurp up the tail like the last noodle in the bowl.

The other day she came in with her mouth full. And sure enough, there was a mouse pup in it. Somehow we managed to get it out unharmed, and it just stood there for a moment looking around, completely bewildered. Then it tore off at top speed.

Sometimes there are wild chases around the house when I try to catch mice that the cat has brought in. I've attached a plastic yoghurt pot to a mop-stick and I use that to capture the mice and release them outside. You have to catch them or they die somewhere and start to stink.

This cat can't stand the smell of the sheep, so she doesn't go into the sheep-house to kill mice. She has completely misunderstood her purpose. She herds in mice, instead of keeping the house clear.

But she isn't as cool as she pretends to be. When I'm away doing my six weeks of pregnancy scanning, she nestles miserably beneath the blanket on my bed every day, which she never does when I'm at home.

Previously, cats were used specifically to combat mouse plagues. Dad would sometimes put a cat in a bag and bring it to the sheep-house at the top of the field. It's built of turf and stone, and the mice lived in its walls. In particularly hard years, there was a risk of them gnawing through the sheep's wool. So a cat would be brought to the sheep-house and given milk to drink while it hunted mice there.

I couldn't say which animals I like best. I love all my animals and, naturally, it's difficult for me to be separated from them. Last year I had to have my old dog Glámur (Moonblaze) put to sleep. He was so dear to me ... it was heartbreaking. The remaining dog, Frakkur (Bold), kept looking for him, completely confused to be suddenly alone.

When I came home from pregnancy scanning that winter, for the first time in fourteen years Glámur wasn't racing to the door to greet me enthusiastically. It was a big change for me, and an incredibly empty homecoming. Glámur was a border collie, like my Frakkur. It's rare for big dogs like that to reach such an age.

At one point in time, there had been some sort of disagreement between Glámur and Frakkur. Frakkur would sometimes have a go at the old dog, and I was worried that this might send Glámur into a seizure. My friend Adda, who had studied dog training in Wales, knew what to do, as she usually does in situations involving animals. She advised me to put crates for the dogs in the laundry room, otherwise tension would continue building between them. I rushed out to buy one, and borrowed the other one from her. These methods aren't really common here in the countryside and Adda was pleased that I was open to experimenting. And it worked. By having the crates, each dog got his own private space in peace from the other, and the tension dissolved. Yes, this is a good example of how I'm happy to try anything, if anyone has suggestions for improvement.

Glámur died in the winter, when the ground was frozen. So I put him in a cardboard box and kept it in the freezer. After he'd been in there a little while, I noticed that the box's lid had moved a bit, giving a glimpse of the dog's fur.

My friend Þór Saari had been doing some volunteer work for me the previous spring, fixing fences. At one point he went to get something out of the freezer. I panicked when I suddenly remembered that he would come across my frozen dog. But Þór never mentioned it, so I hope that he hadn't been surprised or shocked.

Once the ground thawed, Mum and I buried the old dog.

A CHRONICLE OF COUNTRY LIFE

It's very important to me that peace be maintained. This can be difficult when everything can quickly become so personal in our small community.

Here in the countryside, a lot of anger was directed at the residents of one farm because of their interactions with Suðurorka. Things had always been good between Ljótarstaðir and that farm, so I phoned these friends and asked that we try not to let this power-plant issue affect our daily lives. While I was going to try to stop the project by any means possible, I hoped that we could maintain our friendship. They believed that it would be possible to keep the two things separate, and it worked; we kept the peace. They then moved to the north, where I went to visit them last year.

I've always tried to do this, to keep the power-plant issues separate from my daily life. But it became harder with every day that passed. Animosity can't be hidden. Some people stopped greeting me. Others turned away when I drove by. It was really painful the first few times that it happened. I try just to keep going, difficult as it is; try to keep my head held high. As a member of the municipal council, too, I have to be very mindful of how I present myself, and act carefully.

It helps that I'm rather introverted. I have a few very close friends, but in the main I'd say that I remain on conversational terms with others. Introversion is a strong characteristic of people from Skaftafell. Around here, motto number one is, don't draw attention to yourself. Motto number two: don't show your emotions.

I feel like an outsider in this community too. I know that some people find my behaviour presumptuous. Drawing attention to oneself, as I've done in connection with this power-plant business, is looked down upon. And I've willingly done media interviews and spoken at public meetings in order to try to do some good and protect what's mine. In Skaftafell District, a person who does these sorts of things is considered a show-off. In Þingeyjar District, it wouldn't be taken so badly. But here you're taught that if in doubt, you should stick to the old advice: shield your ears and wait for the gusts of scandal to settle.

I often think about Ólafía Jakobsdóttir from Hörgsland in Síða, who was mayor of Skaftá Municipality for many years. She's always been committed to environmental conservation, and not everything that her opponents said about her was kind. One of their oft-repeated comments was: 'That damned old frump never allows anything!'

The Skaftártunga community is a tough one. Life is a hard struggle here. The community over in Síða is much gentler, matching the landscape. I've been lucky enough to have occasionally got to shear sheep with a few of the men from Síða and from Landbrot. When the shearing is finished for the day, they say things like: 'Thanks for today.' And then they hug each other. I was dumb-founded the first time I saw this; I don't think I've ever seen men hug in Skaftártunga. But those guys have real camaraderie.

Here in Tunga, it's more as though you stand hunched by a wall, trying to keep out of the wind. It's safest to try to look meaner than others. Raise your hackles and bare your teeth a bit, just to be safe. There were always tensions here, long before the power-plant issues. This is a community of tough guys. You can't show any sign of weakness. If you do, you'll be walked over.

Over in Síða, people are more patient; they tolerate each other's flaws better. There's also less backbiting.

So it suits me to live on a fairly remote farm. The distance from Snæbýli is just right; and contact with my neighbours there remains friendly and non-interfering. On the other hand, it would be bad to be the only farm in the valley.

All that said, relations between people here in the countryside are good, in that frustration never runs deep. If you're in trouble, everyone will jump in right away and help out. If needed, every single person here would show up with their hammers, tractors and other equipment, ready and willing to assist whomever it might be.

HERDING AND SORTING

I was the first woman to participate in the Skaftártunga round-up on a quad bike. It was in 2004, the year after I got my quad. It was taken as read that I would be herding sheep with such a vehicle, and it's physically demanding to be riding a quad through those difficult highland pastures, which are vast, steep and scored with deep gorges. I was just given help, like any other rookie, and was taught the right paths to take on the quad.

Around here, you're never made to feel like you can't do something because you're a woman. In our local community, it's never been an issue. But the further you go from here, the more you feel that people are surprised about a woman taking on certain tasks.

Of course, when on the quad, whether it's in the highland pastures or anywhere else, you need to be careful and think ahead. It helps that I enjoy riding it. It would have been even better if I'd got myself completely accustomed to it as a kid. There's a definite art to it.

I was fifteen when I first participated in the round-up, so I've been going now for almost a quarter of a century. Before I began using the quad, I went on foot and on horseback. And I feel as if I'm only now getting to know those pastures properly. It's a vast area, the Skaftártunga summer pastures. I couldn't say I'd ever really been up in the mountains, either, until I was fifteen. I'd only gone once to Hólaskjól. It takes many years to get to know that huge area really well.

Yes, I do have a favourite place. It's the lake Hólmsárlón and the adjacent mountains, Svartahnúksfjöll. The Hólmsá River runs from Hólmsárlón, which reaches as far as the Torfajökull Glacier. Many people are familiar with Strútslaug, a hot spring you can bathe in, at the northern end of the lake. This is an utterly unique area; the lake is such an incredibly beautiful colour, which changes according to how much glacial run-off is in it. The water can be sky blue or green, or even reddish brown. It's an amazing place.

Even though I've spent so long here, I can't help but get distracted by the landscape while herding. I often get tempted to hike up a hill just to take a look around. 'Aren't you coming, Heiða?' the walkie-talkie might squawk. And then I have to pretend to be checking on something in particular: 'I don't remember that much water being there last year!'

It's on the year's later round-ups, when there are fewer sheep to gather, that you have a better chance to get to learn your way around the area, and have more time to enjoy the scenery. On those round-ups, it's also possible to return home the same evening. I really don't like sleeping in the hut with twenty other people. It's not my thing to share a mountain hut with a crowd, even if I like the people. I'm a private person, and I like being at home in the evenings in my recliner, and having my own shower and my own bed. There's also something silly about camping in your own backyard. It's such a short distance from Ljótarstaðir, maybe thirty kilometres, although the going can be slow.

My favourite thing about the round-up this year was that my sister Ásta was there. In 1977, she and Habba from Snæbýli became the first women to participate in them. But Ásta hadn't gone since her oldest child was born thirty-four years ago. It was such fun having her there and seeing how much she was enjoying herself. We were also very lucky with the weather. It was like being on a sunny beach somewhere.

Good weather makes a round-up much less stressful. If it really rains, you're almost guaranteed to end up with a 'round-up cold'. On a quad bike, you're always going against the wind and rain; the water pours down your neck and no coverall can keep it out, so you end up soaked to the skin.

It's often rainy and foggy up there. Sometimes we can't do any herding for hours, or even a whole day. It's no use trying to herd if the herders can't see anything, can't even see where the sheep are going. But we try to do so at even the slightest opportunity. It's important that we get as much done as we can on the Friday, so that we can finish the sorting over the weekend. A large group of people, pretty much the same ones every year, comes to help. Thank goodness, because it's an enormous amount of work, sorting out all those sheep. If we had to do it on our own, it would take us forever. But with this many people it always ends up being a really fun weekend, too.

Now we usually take a pre-round-up day to hike up to the highland pastures, just to give ourselves the extra time. But to end up having to hang about in the hut for a whole day in a dark fog is excruciatingly boring. It's such a maddening waste of the day just sitting there, staring into the fog.

Around five to six thousand sheep summer in the highland pastures. A few hundred make their way home early, leaving about five thousand needing herding back. It's one of the largest summer pastures in the country, and we need to comb the whole area to ensure that all the sheep get back home. We herd from the Fögrufjöll Mountains, between the highland lake Langisjór and the Skaftá River, east to Vatnajökull. These pastures are demarcated in the north by the Tungnaá River and in the west by the border between Skaftártunga and Landsveit, which stretches all the way to Torfajökull Glacier and the Hólmsá River. Herding is also done on unfenced land belonging to Ljótarstaðir and Búland.

Going to the highland pastures is all right – herding is fun and the whole thing can be enjoyable – but in a certain way it's like any other project. No better and no worse than any other work. The highland pastures are vital to our livelihood – it's crucial that the sheep go there to graze. In the autumn, the farmers here have to stick together. Whatever disagreements we have at other times, we all have to unite in the autumn, be friends and help each other. And we've always succeeded in doing so.

During this last round-up, as so often before, teen-agers came along to help with the herding. It's great having them. They really make an effort, and it's an excellent learning experience for them. But it's the responsibility of the grown-ups to ensure that the young people have fun and that they're not dragged into our old disputes. We have to remember that we're role models. I find it comes naturally to want to take responsibility for them. I love their company: they're lively and fun, which is how I like things to be, not just in the round-ups but always. After all, there's plenty of time later in life to be uptight with frustration and old age!

The highland pastures are difficult terrain, and our group is extremely tough. Herding means long days over a vast area. The mountains are steep and full of gorges and ravines. It can be very trying for the people on foot, not least because the sheep are no less tough than we herders and even more obstinate!

I find that the sheep differ in obstinacy depending on their region and its terrain. This particular area is conducive to misbehaviour. There are so many ways out and so many opportunities to escape – which the sheep learn that they can do. We farmers here all have a few cheeky bastards and absconders. In Þistilfjörður, where I've helped out herding a few times, the sheep behave completely differently. For instance, it's impos-sible to drive them over water. If they see even the tiniest stream, they'll turn. It's practically headline news if a sheep there crosses water unforced, but in the Skaftártunga pastures the sheep are herded over rivers and streams every day. The round-ups are different too. I really enjoyed herding in Þistilfjörður with a horse and dog. It was a much shorter and easier job than the one here.

I don't take my dogs with me because I haven't got them accustomed to being on the quad bike, and it takes practice – but dogs are of course invaluable for herding the sheep. Ella has two border collie bitches, and she carries them both on her quad. It's wonderful to see. The bitches sit in a half-box at the back of the quad, on a mat, which gives them a foothold on the bike. And they hang on there as Ella rolls along. If a lot is going on, Ella takes them off the quad. You have to look after the dogs, of course; you can't just drive around like mad with them on the back. And it's great to have Ella's bitches on hand; so helpful to be able to send them up the slopes after the sheep. But the days are past when everyone brought their dogs along, whether they were any good or not. I'm glad things have changed because it was a stupid way to treat the poor things, making them sleep outside at night in the autumnal cold. Now we just have a few well-trained dogs on the round-ups, and they sleep inside.

Ella's old Píla (Dart) sleeps with us in the bunk. It's cosy having her there, and soothing to cuddle up to her while falling asleep. Píla was supposed to sleep at our feet, but she sneaked her way up in between us, pushing her paws against one of us and her back against the other, to make more room. So Ella and I are jammed at the edges of the bunk, with the dog in prime place in the middle. She's the most comfortable, but all three of us are perfectly happy.

I always wear rubber shoes – during the round-up as well nowadays – unless it's pouring with rain, or cover-all weather, or if I'm mucking out the sheep-houses. I always used to wear hiking boots during the round-ups, before I discovered why I was so damned tired all the time – I didn't have the strength to lift my boots high enough and was always tripping up because of it. I also had constant joint pain, and my ankles were so sore that I couldn't stand the pressure that the boots put on them. So I switched to rubber shoes all the time. And I still go everywhere in them: all the hikes with my hiking group and wherever else. I do, however, change into hiking boots or rubber boots once it gets to late autumn, perhaps by the third round-up, when there's a risk of snow or ice or frozen ground. In such circumstances, when things are slippery, it's downright dangerous to wear rubber shoes.

This autumn, things went to pot the day before I left for the round-up. I was planning on heading up to the pastures on the Sunday night, because I don't like spending a night longer than I have to in the hut. But at noon that Sunday, the kitchen drain became clogged. It was really bad timing, because the following Friday loads of people would be coming to the corral here at Ljótarstaðir, expecting food and coffee. And the place would be packed all that weekend: nineteen people would be staying at my place during sorting this year.

I rang Siggeir and he rushed out here as fast as he could. We tore up the terrace, almost in its entirety. Then we dug eight metres by hand, taking out pipe after pipe. But we couldn't free the clog before night-fall. I had to leave for the round-up on the Monday. On Tuesday, my neighbour Palli came and took my place on my quad bike, herding for me. When I came home, Siggeir and I continued, until we finally found the blockage, cleaned out the pipes and put them back together, shovelled over them and rebuilt the terrace.

The worst thing is that I'm pretty sure it was my fault from when I dug out around the house to drain and insulate the foundation. I don't think I was careful enough with the angle of the pipes when I reburied them.

The good weather lasted until Friday. It was almost too hot at the home corral, which is something you can't say every year. It's wonderful to have blazing sunshine, and meet friends and relatives whom you might not get to see too often. There are thirty to forty people here for the sorting. And the kids were having a grand old time. There was a buffet of cakes and coffee in the farmhouse, and beer for the people at the corral. Hopefully everyone is as content as can be.

There'll be quite a crowd for lunch, at least twenty people, I guess, once the sheep are all back and before we start the sorting. So we'll need to eat in groups.

Mum prepared the smoked lamb, cured by Valur from Úthlíð. It doesn't get any better, and there are new potatoes from our garden to go with it. And ice cream for dessert. Plenty of nice sweets and lots of brandy to wash it all down with.

Everyone is looking forward to going tomorrow to the Gröf corral for more sorting, and then ending up at the round-up dance at Tungusel. These two nights, people sleep here in the farmhouse, any place they can find: in every available bed, then on mattresses on the floor, in the living room, even under the kitchen table – everywhere, really.

MY FARM AND THE
FIGHT FOR MY LAND

This farm is far more than a business. This is our family home. And everyone with ties to Ljótarstaðir should feel welcome here. They should feel like it's their refuge. It's a huge responsibility to live in such a place and take care of it.

And it's not just my immediate family. Dozens of people have historical connections to Ljótarstaðir. Last summer people came here all the way from Canada to visit the farm – in the rain. Next summer, we'll be holding a family reunion here. If anyone is toying with the thought of trying to take over this farm, they should know that it isn't just like any workplace but is also a family seat, a home and a private space.

To be the only worker keeping this going and continuing this battle while feeling as though I'm being punched in the face over and over and over, on a boat that's being constantly rocked beneath me, can be an almost unbearably heavy burden at times. Everything depends on this one particular worker staying in one piece, on my being able to organize everything and manage all of the endless chores here at the right time, and see to the welfare of my flock and the farm as a whole.

The Suðurorka men have had it far easier. They haven't had to add all kinds of extra meetings to their enormous workload. They haven't had to feel devastated over the thought of their land being taken away from them. They haven't had to experience their neighbours turning away as they drive by.

This contest is incredibly unbalanced. On one side are employees of a company whose job is to meet with the Angling Association, follow up on the studies done here in the Skaftártunga, send emails and visit and put pressure on Parliament. They're paid to pester the people on the expert committees if that's what it takes to implement this project. The steering committee for the master plan was, for instance, sent a letter demanding that Þóra Ellen Þórhallsdóttir, an expert on plant life in the Icelandic highlands and award-winning conservationist, recuse herself from the Búland Power Plant project. The Suðurorka men do all of these things as fully paid work.

On the other side is me, defending my farm, my home and my business on top of a full-time job – which is usually much more than a full-time job. So all my phone calls, my emails, my articles and speeches, my candidacy for a seat on the municipal council, attendance at meetings, my committee work for Vatnajökull National Park are in addition to my incredibly time-consuming full-time job as a sheep farmer and ewe-pregnancy scanner. I get paid a small salary for my public work, but it's tiny considering how much time goes into it, including the time spent driving to meetings.

If this fight continues for years, and involves lawsuits and litigation going all the way to Brussels, I don't know how I'm going to keep going. The odds are that I might bend or crack along the way. Thank goodness for the invaluable support I've had from relatives, friends and others, from all sectors of society, as well as from environmental conservation groups.

And all this is happening after the scientific community deemed it absurd to try to develop power-plant projects at Skaftá because of the enormous environmental damage that they could cause, not least contributing yet further to the terrible wind erosion that already plagues the area. Perhaps my fight – our fight – has been needless. Perhaps too much energy has been spent on something that would never have come about anyway. Now I'll never know.

But the damage is done. Our peace of mind is shattered. Neighbours, friends, relatives, old colleagues have all been pitted against each other and we can't turn the clock back.

For years, I've been tortured by the thought of what I'll do if I lose. I don't think I could bear walking around here after the reservoir was filled. I couldn't imagine seeing it while herding sheep – that filthy puddle in the middle of our green landscape, the result of their annexation of the river.

Some of the people who wish the best for me, especially some of the older people, have said something along the lines that it might be better to make a deal and at least get something out of it. These people were convinced that that's how it would end. The threat of expropriation is big und ugly. The thought is horrendous – of having everything you're responsible for taken away from you.

If the worst happens and my land is taken – the threat of which has been hanging over my head for so long – then I'll take a wrecking ball to my walls and scram. I would see the place as uninhabitable, unfit for human society.

One of the things that I find most unbearable is having these people crawling all over my river and across my land; these people who have come here to destroy my land in order to make money from it. I'm constantly aware of them wading through the river, scaring the geese and disturbing my sheep. And they're allowed to do so. And I who live here, the landowner, am not allowed to kick them off my land.

One big question: how is it that a developer always rears his head when studies are being done, whether it's current measurements or archaeological research? It's unbelievable. It's scandalous that a developer should be the one funding the studies, doing the environmental impact assessment. The experts who came here, such as the ornithologists, were outstanding. I asked them if they would track me down a great auk, which they laughingly said they'd be happy to do. I'm not criticizing the experts. But how can you be reassured with the developer hovering over them? And what about the arrangement that it's the developer who finances the research and selects the engineering firms? How can that be right or fair?

HEIÐA AT A PUBLIC MEETING

Icelandic agriculture is very close to my heart, no less than environmental conservation. As I see it, the two are totally intertwined, as the farmer is entirely dependent on nature for his survival and has a duty, in my view more than in any other profession, to defend it by every means possible.

The activities of the energy industry have done enormous damage to rural communities. Many farmers have lost heart. Those opposed to the power plants are told repeatedly that they're not only standing in the way of progress, but they're also standing in the way of their neighbours being able to utilize their land the way they see fit. This is of course what some farmers have done: sold off their land, or parts of it. But no one can own land in the same way as you own a car. A car is a short-lived machine; you can do with it what you want. I don't own the land. The land owns me. There are heavy responsibilities that come with being owned by all this land . . . and it can be a struggle protecting it from the vultures.

It's nothing but short-sightedness, appropriating
land and destroying it. What gives us the authority to
do that, when life goes on after we're gone? At least I
assume that life will go on after I no longer exist.

Ljótarstaðir has provided for so many people, generation after generation since the eleventh or twelfth
century. And this thousand-year-old farm has been
entrusted to me merely for a few years. Then other
people will come whom this farm will sustain, as it has
always done. It has always done its duty, even after
repeated volcanic eruptions – sustaining flock of sheep
after flock of sheep.

As has my river, the Tungufljót, which flows past my
farm. What would Skaftártunga be without it; what
would my farm be without it? All the kids who grew up
here played by this river, at all times of the year. And
they were planning to take it away, those arrogant
bastards.

HERDING AND SORTING, CONTINUED

On Saturday, the morning before the sorting, all the sheep that don't belong to our farms have to be brought down to the main corral at Gröf. We help each other bring them down there, by tractor and wagon. There are always at least two to three hundred of such sheep. Some of mine always end up at the main corral. We drive those sheep home, and everyone comes back to Ljótarstaðir.

Then the lambs are separated from the ewes. The lambs are allowed to graze in the hayfields, while the ewes are put in the sheep-houses for the night to deal with their grief. They cry out for their lambs, the poor things. It's terribly sad to hear. But I make sure that the lambs are out of earshot of their mothers, and they just go on grazing.

About this time, however, everyone's getting ready for the round-up dance. It's always held at Tungusel, our community centre, and it's always tremendous fun. I guess that around two hundred of us attend the dance.

On the next day, I let the ewes out and try to keep at least a field between them and the lambs so that they don't get back together. Naturally, this is harsh treatment, and the mothers take their separation really hard.

Then the rest of our autumn is devoted entirely to the sheep. We do further round-ups: first, second and third searches, fetching sheep from here and there. September and October are taken up with weighing them, grouping them, moving them about and sending lambs (mainly) to the slaughterhouse. And then there's shearing. For me, autumn easily lasts into November.

SHEARING

Once the round-ups and the slaughtering are finally done, I get everything ready for bringing the sheep in, spread sand on the floor, and then shear them inside. I start shearing the youngest ewes in October, and have usually finished with the whole flock by around mid-November.

Working alone, I can shear around sixty to seventy sheep per day. If I have people to help pull the sheep over to me, I can do a lot more. If I manage to shear all the sheep on the same day that I bring them in, it's a dream, because then they're like marshmallows, dry and puffy. The ewes mustn't be inside for more than one night before being sheared, otherwise their wool gets spoiled and has to be marked as second-rate. It's crucial to keep the wool from becoming moist or wet, so that it doesn't start to get mouldy.

Shearing is such a fast-paced job that there can of course be accidents. One of the things that I hate most is causing an animal pain and suffering. Once I accidentally cut a teat off one of the yearlings. That sheep is still in my flock, and normally bears two lambs, so I have to give one of her lambs to another ewe. It's unusual to keep a sheep with one teat, but I let her live because it was my screw-up and I felt guilty.

I worked for a number of years as a professional shearer; it's well paid and brought me good extra income. It's also incredibly fun, something no one understands until they've done it. There's nothing like the feeling when you switch on the shears and the fleece starts sliding off.

Every autumn, my fingers itch to go back into professional shearing. My sister Ásta was a professional shearer, and my role model. But relatively few women do this, in Iceland at least, and some people found it puzzling that not only did I want to do this work, but that I also enjoyed it and was good at it. I even heard that my shearing work, not to mention my competing in shearing competitions sometimes, is seen as a craving for attention. Some people have bad-mouthed me for it. I seem to provoke some people, unintentionally. In my defence, I found being on the organizing committee for our midwinter feast awfully hard, and it was even worse having to perform skits and songs there.

Electric shears were first used here at Ljótarstaðir some time around 1980. We used them to shear only a small portion of our sheep in late winter. Most of the sheep were shorn in the summer with hand shears. Dad tried his hand at the electric shears, with Mum's help, but as he'd never learned how to do it from anyone it always went horribly, to put it mildly.

Luckily my sister Ásta was a very talented shearer, so much so that she did it quite a bit for others, and sometimes here at home, too. Shortly before my twentieth birthday, the sheep-house at home was insulated and clad with corrugated iron. (As with so much else, Siggeir did this job.) After that we began shearing in the autumn, and I sheared my first sheep in the autumn of 2000, when I was at farmers' college.

After my shearing course that spring, I managed to scrape enough money together to buy a professional machine, which still runs like clockwork now, even after shearing truckloads of sheep. I immediately loved shearing, and wanted to master it. I was completely determined to shear my own sheep, and vowed to get better and better at it.

The following year, I worked as a shed hand, turning the sheep onto their hindquarters for the shearer, and then did the shearing at Snæbýli and Búland when my colleagues Ingi and Gísli took breaks. Then I started accompanying them to farms now and then, and sometimes even sheared on my own. My first big tour was in the spring of 2005, and my last one in the autumn of 2008. I often worked with my friend Helgi Haukur; shearing is twice as fun if you're on a team. We had a great time, joking and goofing around. At one farm, he actually stuffed me into a wool sack – and one of these days, I'm going to get my own back. Ever since stopping shearing professionally I've only done my own sheep, apart from a few times just for fun at other farms, for people I like.

In recent years, I've attended courses given by British teachers, in both Iceland and Scotland, in order to improve my skills. I'm not on my way back into professional shearing though – this is just another of my hobbies.

In 2015, I travelled to Britain to take part in a shearing competition. My main colleagues from Iceland were Hafliði and his wife Gréta Guðný. They're passionate, exacting farmers who met at Hvanneyri, studying for degrees in agriculture. And now they work together on the farm where Guðný grew up in Berufjörður, called Fossárdalur. It's a phenomenally beautiful spot, surrounded by mountains, which you wouldn't expect there. Also on the trip was the multiple Icelandic champion, Julio, and his wife Lilja, from Hávarðsstaðir in Leirársveit . . . not to mention my niece Arndís, my sister Stella's daughter.

Shearing competitions aren't everyday occurrences. There's some talk of making sheep shearing an Olympic event. In the places where I've taken part overseas, for instance in Scotland, the competition facilities (that is, the shearing sheds) are standardized. They have precisely measured sides, the pen is in its place, everything is the perfect height and the shears hang in the right place. You won't find that sort of set-up in Iceland.

In this particular competition in Yorkshire, there were so many talented shearers. I love watching them. Their speed and skills are marvellous: it's great to see how they can shear each sheep in under a minute. Competitive shearers have to be extremely physically fit. Besides shearing, they do lots of physical training and are world-class athletes.

And you're working with living creatures too. Very high penalties are imposed if you harm a sheep, cut or injure it in some way.

The nature of shearing is that the more comfortable the sheep is, the easier it is to shear it. The more comfortable it is, the less it wriggles and kicks. Success is based on the animal being as calm as possible. That can get harder in a shearing competition, when audience members scream and shout their support for their favourite shearer. The announcer can go mad with enthusiasm, too. Not too long ago, Ivan Scott from Donegal set a world record for speed by shearing a sheep in just 37.9 seconds.

There are also competitions for the number of lambs of a specific age shorn in nine hours, and also in eight hours and ten hours. The best competitors can shear seven hundred or more lambs in nine hours.

THE MOTORIST

Getting my quad bike revolutionized my life. It's incredible how much time it saves being able to go everywhere and do everything with it, all that tending to sheep and fences in particular, which I used to have to do on foot or in a slow tractor. And for someone who's always doing sheep work on her own, the quad has become my most necessary tool on the farm. Apart from that, I just really enjoy it. I'm an incurable petrolhead. My dream is to own a motorcycle. And a sports car.

HEIÐA AT A POETRY MEET-UP

I've always loved machinery, and I'm pretty sure that will always be the case. For the longest time, I've madly wanted to own a two-seater Mercedes Benz, and then of course a motorcycle would be even better. But seeing as neither fits directly into Ljótarstaðir's budget, I've begun to realize that there'll probably be some side effects if I ever really do intend to own hot rods such as those. And, well, I'm not getting any younger. Although maybe tonight's the night to do something about that:

Though my age might lessen my chance,
I think that tonight I'll head to the dance
and try just for fun
to find that someone
who likes a bike, Benz and romance.

THE SHEEP IN AUTUMN

Empathy doesn't exist in sheep. You can see this in how harshly the ewes shove and knock away other ewes' lambs. As soon as a sheep breaks its leg or falls ill, it's at risk of being trampled. It's completely different with horses, which immediately give way if there's a weaker animal, such as a small puppy, nearby. But maybe it's for the best that sheep aren't very sensitive, considering how they're treated: made to have lambs every spring, which are then taken away from them in the autumn.

It's not an enjoyable time when the lambs are taken from their mothers. It's crucial to make sure that the lambs and ewes can't hear each other. I shut the ewes inside to start with. It usually takes about five days for the separation to be complete. On the other hand, the reactions vary greatly between individual sheep and lambs. Some lambs just bleat two or three times, and then think: oh, okay, she's gone! Others hang around by the fences and continue searching. The same goes for the ewes. Some are devastated and look for their lambs for some time. Others don't.

Nevertheless, by September the lambs are nearly full-grown, and are ready to be separated. One thing that happens naturally during early autumn's cold spells and storms is that ewes sometimes simply head home and leave their lambs up in the highlands. That's something they most certainly wouldn't do in July.

Selecting the right animals for breeding can be a tricky business too. You always try to choose the very best gimmers, of course, especially according to ancestry.

Watching the sheep going to the slaughterhouse is always hard. Worst is when older ewes go, when they're nine years old or thereabouts. You don't get paid much for them, but at least they're slaughtered professionally. It's tough having to load them onto the truck simply because they're old and can't have lambs any more; you've got to know them, and they've stopped acting idiotically. Sheep can be kind of loopy until they're three or four years old. These older sheep are easy to handle, and they know how everything works – all the gates, for instance. They're well behaved and act sensibly, know how things are done, know you and trust you. And then they're put down. It's harsh.

ON THEIR BACKS

One danger to the sheep, particularly in the autumn, is rolling over onto their backs. It's the lambs that are most at risk, as they've grown big and fat and have broad backs. It happens mainly after it rains – when they dry out they start itching, and then they try to roll over to scratch their backs, as they could do easily when they were little. But then they discover that they're no longer able to get back on their feet again.

On their backs, they're fair game for the ravens that are never far away. If ravens come across such a catch, they sometimes peck the eyes out of living lambs or sheep, which can then bleed to death through their eye sockets. Or a raven might peck a hole in the overturned sheep's belly. That means half-digested food can get into the animal's abdomen, dooming it to die of fever and peritonitis. I've even tried giving a lamb that this happened to a huge dose of penicillin, but it didn't work.

I've seen this sort of horror inflicted many times. I found it pretty indicative of how far removed people have got from their origins when, in some fancy-pants magazine, I saw clip art of two ravens on the wall above the headboard of a master bed. One was swooping down with outstretched claws, while the other hovered in the air, waiting to get its own claws and beak into the prey. I would never have been able to sleep under pictures of this bird in such horrid, menacing positions. I would probably have had nightmares about the bastards pecking out my eyes.

I was on my way to the highland pastures with Ella the day that I saw this photo, and it upset me so much that I couldn't stop talking about it the whole day. Imagining those chic people lounging there blissfully with their kids, beneath the outstretched claws of the raven.

A DIFFERENT SORT OF
ROUND-UP DANCE

My Uncle Sverrir wrote an ode to Skaftártunga, which has since become the anthem of the Tunga community. It's often sung at gatherings, such as sorting at the corrals. The first verse goes as follows:

Skaftártunga, fair and bright,
adorning this our land so dear.
Its stories shared, to folk's delight,
some forgotten, some still clear.
Its fair slopes, wooded, catch the eye,
glancing with a lustrous sheen.
Its vast expanses, when viewed nigh,
reveal wondrous gardens green.

One verse has these lines:

Widely streams here ever run,
and Tungufljót so strongly flows
bringing households light like sun,
and giving cheeks their cheery glows.

Now it was time for the round-up celebration – and who should show up at the pre-dance party but the Suðurorka man. He'd recently published an article in which he tried to appropriate Sverrir's verses for the energy industry. But Sverrir's lines were, of course, describing a different, less harmful technology – the construction of smaller, home generators, of which my fellow inhabitants of Tunga were important pioneers. This twisting of our anthem didn't do much to increase Mr Suðurorka's popularity around here.

The atmosphere was great, full of energy and happiness . . . the dance was just about to start, and I was still on such a high after all the effort in the mountains and at the corral. Plus, the alcohol made me a bit more impulsive than usual.

At that point we were in the sheep-house at Borgarfell. It's a brand-new, elegant building, where a party is held in the evening after sorting, with people singing and harmonica music to their heart's content. We were standing in the middle feeder aisle, the pens on both sides. And I was laughing and joking with my sister Fanney and some friends. Then we started singing 'Skaftártunga, fair and bright'. When we finished the song, the Suðurorka man nearby presumptuously started in on it again, when he had no business singing it at all. I didn't join in. And anger started boiling up inside me – visibly, no doubt, like in a cartoon. I held my tongue until I could no longer contain myself, and burst out: 'I'm going to kill this bastard!'

Then I started walking towards him with slow, heavy steps. Fanney and our friends called out after me:

'Come back here! Come back!' But I kept going until they rushed over, grabbed me from both sides and forced me out to the car.

I was so angry that I could barely see; literally blinded by anger. They pushed my head down and squeezed me into the car. For some time, I didn't say a word. Then we went to the dance, where I quickly recomposed myself after my fit of anger. Luckily, the Suðurorka man didn't show his face there.

This shocked Fanny, because she'd never known me to start trouble when drinking before. But she also knows that I'd never make empty threats. If they hadn't stopped me, I would have grabbed him and toppled him into the sheep pen. It would have been bad. I'm very grateful to them for stopping me.

I'm not a violent person. I never get grumpy, whine or puke when drinking. 'There's happiness in my bottles.' Fanney and I saw this fine expression in an obituary: there's definitely happiness in my bottles. It's undeniable that some people's bottles can be full of tears and fights and anger. Alcohol does that to some people. Of course, I've seen a lot of ugly drunkenness, while other people can get downright jubilant with drink.

I've never been a heavy drinker. When I'm letting my hair down, I take good care not to embarrass myself, and also watch out that I don't drink to the point of helplessness – to others' embarrassment and my own ridicule, as my old dad used to say. On the other hand, I have to admit it looks like I'll never grow out of play-fighting – which can often end up with my being picked up and carried out over someone's shoulder. I've got to stop this now that I'm almost middle-aged. But as for being ready to punch people while drinking – that's happened only this one time.

I wasn't the only one there annoyed with the Suðurorka man. When he asked one of the Borgarfell brothers, who was transporting people to the round-up dance, if he could give him a lift there, the brother replied with a flat no.

This round-up dance was so much fun. It ended with me and two other girls bursting into the room where my neighbour lay fast asleep, and we jumped into bed with him and poked him in the ribs with a teaspoon. And there he lay with the three of us on top of him fully dressed, along with the stuffed ram's head that one of us had brought along, just to be safe.

WINTER

HEIÐA AT A POETRY MEET-UP

People are always going on and on about how everyone should have children; that more children are needed to keep the schools and health clinics running. They tried to sell me this idea when I was younger. And normally, it was presented along these lines:

Playing, so quiet and sweet.
Laughing, so good and discreet.
Always obedient, bouncy and bright.
A farm full of kids – such a delight!

But now that I've been here and there, and have watched my sister's own rug rats grow up, I find this to be a more realistic depiction:

No, those kids there are really not nice,
they cough and they spew, they're covered in lice.
They don't do their schoolwork, those little
    snobs,
they lie, drink and smoke; such horrible slobs.

2 DECEMBER 2015

Last night there was a howling snowstorm . . . there's
ice everywhere. The power lines up here have often
snapped in such conditions and the fences get badly
damaged. I even had to knock ice off and from around
my Lux with a shovel, which took longer than I thought
it would – and I was wearing only light clothing, no
wool socks. It was so cold that my hair froze into strips
and it was still wet when I went out. But I was going to
be late for a meeting in Klaustur and there was no time
to spare.

7 DECEMBER

I've been anxious ever since I heard the weather forecast. And now, the weather's been awful since this
morning. Luckily, my flock is unaware of the terrified
farmer who can't eat or sleep. I'm not afraid for myself,
but that the sheep-houses might be torn apart, leaving
the sheep unprotected.

Many farmers don't react like this. Storms have little
effect on them.

I've been living on my own here for almost a month
now, because Mum is in hospital. But there's no room
for indulgences such as fear of the dark in such storms,
because the real threat is so great. If the electricity goes
off, though, it's awful being alone in the darkness. Just
now it was out for an hour but, thank goodness, it came
on again. It was terrible not knowing when the electricity would return . . . despite my having a flashlight, of
course, and plentiful candles, and Fífill as well.

As a child, and for some time afterwards, I was afraid
of the dark. It's not a good idea to frighten children
with stories of bogeymen or ghosts. There are still
traces of that fear left in me now, I know, but I can force

myself to stay calm, and it's not a bad idea to remind myself that there's more reason to fear the living than the dead.

It's darkest now, at the beginning of December, but the days will have grown longer again by the end of February. I don't dread the winter, but by the end of November I'm pretty tired and looking forward to January, when I try to take some time to rest and recharge my batteries for all the toil of the coming year.

There are always plenty of jobs needing doing, of course. December is insemination month, when the rams are put together with the ewes. Christmas preparations also take some work. Then everything goes into overdrive in February and March: six weeks of pregnancy scanning all over the country, plus the time-consuming preparations for it, which involve detailed organization and scheduling involving communication with over two hundred farms, as well as preparing myself, my equipment and sanitation supplies, and all the clothes I'll need – amounting to twelve coveralls and more.

As far as the darkness goes, there are two farms in this valley, and I like seeing the lights at Snæbýli, a little less than two kilometres away. I would feel uncomfortable not being able to see them. It's also very reassuring having the cat and dogs too. My Fífill in particular is a true ghostbuster.

When I was little, there were no exterior lights here at Ljótarstaðir. Dad was against lighting up the sky, as he phrased it. But I disagreed with him about that, as about most things. It didn't take me long to install lighting after I started having a say in things here. I've now got it decently lit up outside, and can see quite well from all the way down at the equipment storage shed to the upper sheep-house.

There's a little fenced path that runs from here to the sheep-house wall, so I can hold onto the wire if need be, or support myself on the fence if the weather's fierce enough to topple me. I've had to crawl that last bit when the weather was at its worst, or when the ground was solid ice.

According to the forecast, this is going to be the worst of it now. It's been crazy since six o'clock. The blasts come in waves. It should get calmer around eleven. Then it's supposed to start blowing from the south some time tonight. But the direction doesn't matter that much, it's just that the forecast is so bad tonight.

We haven't had such bad weather here for years. I remember storms like this when I was a kid and a teenager. But the weather's been good, in general, ever since I took over here.

I've been talking on the phone, and now I can't concentrate on anything. I can't eat or drink and am walking around half-dazed. The young dog doesn't take any notice, and the old one is hardened to it.

It would be impossible to stand upright in it out there now. If the forecast is right and it calms down before midnight, I'll go outside, start the tractor and shine its lights on the outside of the sheep-houses to see how things look. When the weather's crazy like this, I'm too chicken to try climbing onto the rooftops to see if anything's coming loose. It's frightening enough to go out there at all . . . and there's not much you can do, anyway, if it were all to start blowing away.

I was too stressed last night to sleep more than half an hour and now I'm running purely on adrenaline. It's hardly smart behaviour, exhausting myself before the day's work; I mean, being dead tired if I had to respond to difficult circumstances.

Naturally, I have to think about reorganizing feeding times if the forecast is really bad. This time, it was pretty clear that I wouldn't be able to open the sheep-houses for two days; it's impossible to open the big doors against the wind, to put in hay bales with the tractor. I managed to feed the sheep twice, put hay everywhere inside, so it's fine. But there's no way out of feeding them twice a day and putting hay in once every three days.

In general, this isn't a terribly windy place, except for last winter. On the other hand, it snows a lot up here, so I often have to dig myself out of the farmhouse, and into the sheep-houses.

The sheep-houses are old and therefore not that sturdy. If they collapse, the sheep will be in danger. These living beings need to be respected, and their welfare ensured. I have to make sure that they don't suffer, aren't injured. As I said, I'm not afraid for myself, but that the houses will be damaged, that the sheep will be vulnerable.

A single person feels so tiny in such mad weather. No one can control the forces of nature. But as Halldór Laxness says in *Independent People*, it all works out somehow, even if we doubt it at times.

One day I'm going to live in a sturdy house in some village in the countryside and not be responsible for five hundred lives. And it won't be bad, being able to pop down to the shop to pick up the jar of spice that I need for cooking supper.

I also want to live abroad somewhere. Maybe in Britain. Or just wherever the rock and roll is.

When I was at school in Selfoss in 1997, we were hit hard on the first of November by an absolutely horrendous blizzard. We lost sixty sheep, and there were huge losses elsewhere in the district. I took three days out of school to help, and came home the following weekends as well, in order to keep searching. The search area is vast, with difficult terrain, and even within the fenced pastures there are loads of ravines.

We were still finding sheep alive in drifts up to three weeks after the storm. They can survive on their own fat reserves for that long. It's an awful experience dragging half-dead and dead sheep out of the snow. Absolutely horrendous. And the morale here on the farm was terrible.

I blamed myself for not insisting on a round-up before I went to Selfoss on the Sunday. The damage from losing those sheep was more psychological than economic. I felt that I failed my animals. I was supposed to have ensured their safety.

Since then, I've always kept my guard up in autumn. I keep a close watch on the weather forecasts. And as soon as the weather looks dicey, I herd the sheep into the houses. It's just part of the deal of living on a heath farm like this. Even if the forecast is just rain, and it can do nothing but rain in the lower parts of this area, it can easily turn into wet or blowing snow up here at these two highest farms, Ljótarstaðir and Snæbýli.

It's the same for all farmers. The worst is if something happens to the animals – if they get lost in a storm, if an animal is sick or injured.

MATING SEASON

When an older gentleman once recited a poem of proposal to me at a poetry meet-up, he got this verse about a ram lamb in return:

I didn't crawl out of the cradle today.
If it's my farming skills you wish to test,
I've been at it long – and therefore can say:
the ram lamb eats light, but clearly humps best.

Rams are incredibly annoying creatures. I've had to reduce the size of my ram pens more than once the closer it gets to mating season, to prevent them from taking such long run-ups when fighting, those knuckleheads.

Rams usually don't live longer than three years. By then, they've sired enough offspring and are fully tried. It's better to use younger rams, which will outdo their fathers. Whereas ewes live much longer: nine years or so.

Tame rams are particularly annoying. They become extremely demanding. Want to be petted all the time. Shove you to get attention. Crazy numbskulls!

And it's a pain in the arse when you weigh barely seventy kilos in your coverall and shoes to shear walloping, hundred-kilo rams. It's manageable if they're well behaved, but one simply deciding to stretch its neck once knocked me into the wall, and another deciding to stand up without warning laid me out flat. I rarely ever sweat much while shearing, but you could wring a bucket of sweat from my clothes after I've shorn a few fully-grown rams.

I have an old ram-shearing poem that goes like this:

The rams, they finally lost their tough fight,
and with that the wool from off their backs went.
The struggle they'd put up was truly a sight;
they left the good shearer bruised up and spent.

I can't handle the rams. They're stronger than me. What I say about them is best understood in light of that.

I've finally learned my lesson: older women should definitely avoid dealing with rams if there are younger people around. In the last sorting, I told my nephew: 'Look, Ármann, there's a ram!' And the dear boy rushed off to get it.

MY DAILY ROUTINE

I start work around eight in the morning, almost every day, all year round. I wake up around seven and take an hour for myself before I go to work. Except of course during lambing, when I go straight from bed to the sheep-houses.

I don't really like going straight out like that. The hour that I take under ordinary circumstances is very important to me, and I often wake up a bit earlier just to make sure that I have it.

I start by taking Frakkur and Fífill out for a walk, and then I feed them. Then I have some coffee and breakfast. After that, during the winter, I go to feed the sheep. The feeding takes about an hour if I don't have to put hay in the barn. When I put hay bales in with the tractor, once every three days, it takes longer.

After the feeding, I turn to other chores or go to meetings – which there are a lot of in the autumn and winter months, and which you have to attend no matter the weather. At the end of the day, there's feeding again. Feeding has to be done every day, whether it's Christmas

Day or whatever. If I'm going to be away from the farm, I have to get someone to do it for me. Most often, it's not a problem, but I hate bothering people so I try to do as little of that as possible.

Sheep farming is different from dairy farming in that there are a few months per year when there are no animals at home needing daily care. Dairy farmers are tied to their cows morning and evening every day of the year.

Most days, I make a work plan, which I need to stick to in order for everything to go smoothly. I always know what I'm going to do the next day. That's essential to me, because I get stressed if things are up in the air. It's okay if I want to take things easy for a day, perhaps because I'm expecting visitors. But I don't like changing my plan, even if I'm good at finding solutions for unexpected problems – especially as I can't just stand here gaping, waiting for someone from the insurance company's breakdown service to show up. Naturally, I like it best when I can stick to a specific task until it's finished. But as a solitary farmer, that's not always possible.

My work methods have become more and more routine over time. I work best by regimen; by taking food and coffee breaks, and preferably avoiding working in the evenings. I always find it frustrating if I get behind schedule.

It's still common in the countryside, at least on this farm, for the day to be divided according to meal and break times: breakfast, ten o'clock coffee, lunch, afternoon coffee, dinner. Coffee and mealtimes are honoured and used for orientation. I decide to finish a specific job either before lunch, or before afternoon coffee, or before dinner. I'm also like a mink in how I need to eat every few hours.

HEIÐA AT A POETRY MEET-UP

I own a ram named Laukur (Onion), who is unusually easy to deal with. It's because of his docility that he's still around. He's easy to lead, and pretty much his only job these days is to walk around with me in the sheep-houses four mornings in December and sniff out the ewes that are in heat. But he only gets to have a whiff, and I yank on his rope if he starts getting any notion of finishing the business himself. I'm sure he finds me pretty unfair on those days.

I wake up my old Laukur while the other rams
    still rest.
He's better than those stallions, see, he doesn't
    strain his lead.
But when he catches warm ewe scent, restraining
    him is best,
though Laukur doesn't like that I don't let him
    spill his seed.

CHRISTMAS

In the run-up to Christmas, it's my tradition to wash the whole house with soapy water. I spend days scrubbing the walls, up and down. I find such cleaning jobs god-awful boring, but I like having clean things around me, so I'll do it if there's no one else to help, whether at Christmas or any other time.

I put up Christmas lights on the farmhouse and sheep-houses at the beginning of December. I like to decorate before Christmas, and I just made my own advent wreath for the first time. It came out pretty well. I really enjoy Christmas, and always stock up with loads of food and sweets.

Fanney and María Ösp have come here for Christmas the last sixteen years. They usually arrive on 22 December. My cousin Addi is also here most Christmases. On the Feast of St. Þorlákur (23 December), we go to the forest at Giljaland and choose a fir tree about one and a half metres high and take it home with us. That evening, we cook hot dogs at home. After decorating the Christmas tree, we have hot cocoa and gingerbread biscuits.

On Christmas Eve morning, my sister Ásta and her son Ármann Daði come over to exchange gifts and have biscuits and cakes and shots of Baileys, and then we have almond porridge for lunch. For dinner on Christmas Eve we have warm smoked lamb, which Valur from Úthlíð cures in his smokehouse.

Mum does all the cooking here. I'm hopeless at it, but that said, I wouldn't starve to death next to a barrel of salted meat, as one clever woman said of her husband. Lamb and mutton are of course staples here, and I like them in all different variations. Our lamb is so good that even I can't screw it up completely by frying or boiling it. That's a real accomplishment, which says far more about the meat than me.

I'm amazed that the increased numbers of tourists in this country haven't dramatically raised the demand for Icelandic lamb. It must have to do with poor marketing; in stores you don't see lamb labelled prominently in any language but Icelandic. And I've been to a restaurant in a flourishing sheep-farming district where no other kind of meat was on the menu but very un-Icelandic turkey.

As María Ösp's birthday is on 25 December, we tend to celebrate it most often on the 26th. Fanney and María Ösp then spend the time between Christmas and New Year at home in Hveragerði.

Christmas is a very pleasant time for me. Constant eating. Plenty of biscuits and cakes. I can bake, and do it really well, despite my day-to-day cooking being the way it is.

Christmas for me, as for so many others, also means gobbling down loads of sweets and chocolates. I particularly like Quality Street. I also watch a lot of TV. But it so happens that I've seen the beginning of lots of movies and the end of very few. There's something so festively cosy about falling asleep over movies. I have a huge sweet tooth even when it's not Christmas. I'm allowed to treat myself – after all, I don't smoke, get drunk only twice a year and have stopped taking snuff. Except when I meet a special snuff-mate. You can find them all over the place. Well, everyone's got to die from something.

Christmas lights glowing, outside is snow,
as I'm smiling the peacefulest smile I can make,
before pleasantly dreaming the best thing I know:
that I'm swimming in wonderful sweets when I
    wake.

I've been here alone on the farm since Mum went into hospital in November. We hoped that she would be able to come out back here for Christmas, but she wasn't allowed. When Mum went to Hveragerði to have her knee aspirated, she developed a bad infection immediately afterwards and has stayed in hospital ever since. She's doing better, but can't use her bad leg very much.

I find it just fine, being here by myself. Some people might call it lonely, but I'm a loner. I like talking to the animals. I wouldn't want to be here without the animals, though.

As a child, I was reclusive. That's not necessarily my nature, but it was because I had no other choice. I got used to being alone. Then in the summer, the other kids would come and everything would change.

CHILDREN AND CHILDLESSNESS

Linda was six years old when she started coming to Ljótarstaðir, and spent ten summers with my family. Now I love spending time with Linda and her family. She and her husband met when they were young, and they have three great kids. They represent a kind of reality, and my connection with them is valuable as it allows me to see how well this arrangement can work, even if it isn't for me.

It's a luxury to have her kids here with me from time to time and to be entrusted with them unreservedly.

'Yes, go in the tractor with Heiða, then!' 'Okay, onto the quad with Heiða. Put your hat on first!'

I think that I've always known that I didn't want to have children. I flinch at the thought of attempting to bring another person mentally and physically intact into adulthood. I'm afraid that I would just raise another nut-job like me. One thing that's certain is that it's easy to ruin a child. And things feel even more messed up nowadays, in so many ways . . . kids and the Internet and what they see there is a particular problem.

But it's not just the difficulties of the parental role that make me hesitate; there are so many things that I want to do more than taking care of a child or children, with all the time and the attention required for that to be done properly.

There's a compulsion to fit all people into the same mould. A tendency to think that if someone is different they can't possibly be okay. I'm thirty-eight years old, and people are still trying to convince me that having a baby would be the best thing that could happen to me. Okay, fine, that may have been the best thing that happened to the person trying to do the convincing, but it doesn't mean that it applies to everyone. I am of course a lost sheep – soon to be forty and not knowing whether I'm coming or going. I have no idea what I want!

Even my sisters put me under a lot of pressure to augment the human race. I finally ended it by saying to them: 'Don't you think I would have just had a baby a long time ago if that had been my plan?' Then they stopped bringing it up.

Even when I was little, I questioned the whole children thing, although it was clearly assumed then that I would have them someday. I never got it. I always thought oh, am I really supposed to have a baby? Why am I supposed to have a baby?

HEIÐA AT A POETRY MEET-UP

Well, here you go, I have a New Year poem, but it's neither positive nor fun. It's definitely not a pretty poem either; in fact, it's kind of disastrous. It's written in a female voice, but it could apply to both sexes, as far as its content is concerned.

With fireworks scare every horse in the land.
Make resolutions you'll never embrace.
Throw up around five, nearly too drunk to stand,
and drag the next idiot back to your place.

NEW YEAR

Every January, I try to take it as easy as possible and gather my strength for the rest of the year. My most strenuous time of the year is coming: six weeks of ewe-pregnancy scanning all over the country.

These two things actually work now, hibernating in January and then travelling. During my first years here, neither would have been an option. I was on the verge of losing it from stress and maybe my only relaxation would be a New Year's dance.

But in the last few years, I've gone abroad, to shearing competitions in Scotland and England, as well as to visit Adda at the farm in Wales where she was learning dog training. I've gone on advent trips with Fanney and María. And many years ago, I went with my cousin Kolla to South America.

For the first month of the year, I try to do as little as possible other than the feeding. I allow myself to sit down in the evenings with a book and maybe a bowl of sweets. I spend most time by far in my recliner next to the radiator in the kitchen. Often my old kitty used to come and curl up with me as I read. I'm always hoping that my new kitty will start doing the same. A winter's night with a book is the best. Surrounded by stillness in my own mountain palace. Maybe stars and the moon; and every now and again the world's most spectacular display of Northern Lights.

PREGNANCY SCANNING

Ella and I are among the pioneers in pregnancy scanning of ewes in Iceland. When Ella first learned of this technology from a Norwegian man who'd been here doing scanning, she asked me whether we shouldn't just dive in and do it. So we invested in a sonar scanner. The two of us attended a weekend course held by this Norwegian, and learned the techniques. The following year, we sharpened our skills at another course in Hamar in Norway. That was back in 2004, so this is my thirteenth year doing pregnancy scanning.

After the first course, Ella and I practised the techniques we learned in the sheep-house at Úthlíð every evening for ten days, scanning the same ewes over and over. That year, there were few farms that utilized our service, but word soon spread, and things took off. By 2008–09, we were fully booked.

Now I do scanning at over two hundred places all over the country, most often on farms, but also for people who keep a few sheep in urban areas. For the last few years, Ella has solely been scanning in our area in the south. We've also trained another pregnancy scanner, our dear friend Logi. He and I each have our own separate equipment, but we work together taking appointments, organizing and advertising. Ella and I, on the other hand, used to travel and do the scanning together. It is of course much easier to work with someone else, and covering all those areas goes quicker. It's also just much more fun to be on the road with someone else, and Ella and I always had a brilliant time together.

The scanning makes a great difference to farmers, revealing to them how many lambs the ewes are carrying and thereby helping them to better organize lambing, arrange things more efficiently. It's all about moving lambs between ewes and ensuring that all healthy ewes have two lambs with them for the summer – that an extra lamb is taken from a ewe with three lambs and given to a ewe with only one.

Part of this arrangement also has to do with the feeding of the sheep. The ewes with three lambs will need more than those with one. By reducing the amount of hay and feed enhancer given to those with one lamb, you reduce the risk of the single lamb growing so large in the ewe's womb that it will be problematic to deliver.

One of the best things about this job is how well received it is. Scanning works to maximize the productivity of each sheep, and it doesn't take many lambs to pay for the ultrasound gel.

Naturally, though, mistakes can occur, as in every human endeavour. Pregnancy scanning requires enormous concentration, and the quality of the scans can be uneven. Many factors come into play. Fighting a snowstorm and shovelling snow half the night does nothing to sharpen my concentration. If the sheep are unruly, nervous and jumpy, that works against me too. The same goes if their stomachs are too full: the foetuses aren't as clear on the scans and sometimes they aren't the right age for scanning, either. If time is tight and things are hectic, that too can ruin your focus.

All day, every day of the six-week tour, you're looking at sonar scans of lamb foetuses. I scan twelve to thirteen hundred sheep per day. I start at eight in the morning and usually don't stop until around eight in the evening. Every sheep is herded into an iron cage that I bring with me. A man here in Iceland made it for me, but the measurements for it were taken in Norway. I also have a specially made, low iron stool, and then of course the sonar equipment.

It was terribly difficult the first few years because nobody knew what we were getting into. Methods had to be invented for herding the sheep properly inside the sheep-houses, as it's extremely important for the scanner to have a steady stream of sheep. It also matters where the cage is placed. At first the farmers had no idea about these procedures and how to help. Now everyone knows what to do.

The cage always needs to be put in the same spot in the sheep-house, because it goes so slowly if you have to move the sonar or herd the sheep past it. That also increases the risk of accidents with the equipment, which must never happen – it could cost me millions of krónur. The only times that I get seriously upset during scanning is if a sheep comes too close to the machine.

Once or twice a sheep has jumped on the machine, but luckily, it turned out okay. If the equipment were to be broken in the middle of a scanning tour, it would be catastrophic. It would take so long to replace it. I would lose out on both that money and my income from the cancelled tour. So that's the only major cause for stress in this business – well, also if you can't get any coffee, of course!

Conditions are difficult and the scanning itself is uncomfortable in general. You sit very low on the sheep-house floor and suffer various aches and pains – you're always at risk of developing tendonitis and muscle inflammation – from doing those constant repetitive movements with the sensor. Added to which, there's the risk of a sheep knocking into you, or worse, a ram. Careful as I am, I've had near accidents twice. Once was when a ram suddenly rushed over and shoved his way under the sheep in the pen, taking my shoulder with him but leaving my hand holding the sensor stuck in the ram's horn at the front of the cage – for one long, terrifying moment, I was convinced that my arm was broken.

For me to do my job properly, it's very important that the people on the farms are experienced in handling sheep; that they're moved continuously and smoothly. And that those bloody rams are kept under control!

In this assembly-line work, you get cold and hungry and are often desperate to go to the toilet. But I've finally learned to ignore my body's signals: I know that this will eventually come to an end. By now, I know that I'm not going to die in this sheep-house, which sometimes seemed possible in my first years doing it. I know that soon I'll be back in the car where it's warm, and where I'll have music and chocolate; and then I just get on with it and it all rolls right along.

I now know that even a sheep-house of twelve hundred sheep will eventually be finished. There's actually just one farm with such an enormous flock and luckily, it's a very nice farm, with fun people. It takes me a whole long day to scan the sheep there.

The same goes for washing the cage out with ice-cold water. At first I thought my hands would fall off. Now I don't let it get to me. It's just temporary; it's all going to be all right. As soon as I've put on my wool mittens, I start feeling better. Sometimes I put them on before I've taken off my coverall.

This job doesn't just involve moving the cage and the scanning equipment between places, putting the cage in its place and starting to count – I also have to clean everything thoroughly at every farm following the scanning, and scrub the cage and the stool, and so on. Of course, I have a veterinary permit for this job. I'm very serious about cleaning everything well between farms and changing my protective clothing. I absolutely must not be the cause of infections spreading between farms due to negligence. And we're so diligent that it won't happen. Sometimes I feel as if people don't realize the importance of this element in my job.

Every square centimetre of my Lux is plotted out when I'm on a tour – there are extra mittens and bala-clavas in every corner. I bring ten to twelve coveralls with me so that I have more than enough for changes. I put on a new coverall at each farm to keep from carrying any infections on my clothing. Luckily, everyone is extremely helpful, willing to wash clothing for you and so forth.

During scanning, it's an added stress constantly being interrupted by my phone. I have to answer immediately, even in the middle of things. If I didn't, the messages would just pile up and I would have an even harder time sticking to my strict schedule. But it's hardly ideal answering the phone with one hand and holding the sensor in the other.

Some people have told me that I'm only doing this because I enjoy roaming around more than being at home. It isn't fair to put it like that, because this bothersome part-time job is crucial for keeping Ljótarstaðir running. This work brings me an income that makes a considerable difference. But it's been a privilege to get to know farmers and their helpers all over the country. I stay at a lot of the same farms year after year. Sometimes I stay for several nights at the same farm if it's suitable distance-wise and particularly good friends live there.

The scanning season falls in the middle of winter, meaning I have to expect every kind of weather on my travels. But I fight my way onward through all the storms and difficult road conditions, because all my careful planning and organization collapses if the timing goes awry.

At worst, I have to dig my way onward. I remember once being stuck on an impassable road in a white-out in the southern part of the Westfjords, and hearing on the car radio that crews were working on clearing the road on Klettsháls Pass. Ella was outside shovelling; we'd been doing so for a few hours and were on the verge of freeing the car. And then after we'd shovelled and jostled and spun and pushed and shovelled some more, the snowplough suddenly showed up. Typical!

Pregnancy scanning is particularly satisfying because it's work that I can dive into and finish. I don't like having to walk away from an unfinished job, which is something that can occur often in farming.

Yes, since you ask, I do have a favourite district. I love Strandir. That's my promised land. I really like the fine people and I feel good there. I always experience a feeling of loss when I leave. The sheep in Strandir are big and beautiful, a special hornless breed. These sheep are very productive and their lambs are heavy, because they're so well taken care of.

In and of itself, travelling the country for six weeks is a good thing for me. It's the same as going abroad. Pregnancy scanning is good schooling for this remote heath farmer. My world expands. I feel as if the walls are shrinking on me if I stay at home for too long.

When I was growing up, I definitely felt how the world at Ljótarstaðir could be quite small – it expressed itself sometimes in a kind of narrow-mindedness and even prejudice. I absolutely cannot stand prejudice of any sort, especially against immigrants or homosexuals. Prejudice and chauvinism are among the worst things I know of.

HEIÐA AT A POETRY MEET-UP

During my tours around the country doing shearing and pregnancy scanning, I find it comforting, through my various crises, to send my sisters verses, especially as I can almost always rely on a speedy response.

On one scanning tour, Ella and I stayed at a certain farm located at the shore of a certain fjord in the Westfjords. The whole night that we were there, I had terrible nightmares about ghosts, which left me grey, sleep-deprived and shivering the next morning. When I told Ella about it, however, she just snickered and said that she herself had slept like a rock in the next room – and every year since then, she's demanded that we stay at that farm.

The following year, then, we arrived there around dinnertime – I was a bundle of nerves and Ella was grinning. And what do you know – just as I was dozing off, I could swear that I heard an oystercatcher calling through the open window. It was the third of March, in the middle of winter in the Westfjords. 'So the nightmare begins – and now that bastard is mimicking an oystercatcher,' was my thought as I furiously slammed the window shut. And then I had another sleepless night. At the breakfast table, the farmer was in the best of moods and said: 'Well, girls, you certainly brought spring with you; I just saw an oystercatcher here on the beach.'

After Ella had stopped laughing, I sent my sisters this poem:

My nerves in uproar,
I cried 'Nightmares, no more!'
And from my bed fled,
filled with the dread
of a new-landed bird on the shore.

Soon afterwards, Fanney sent me this reply:

Your Skaftafell bravery must hollow ring
and you'll need a good comrade to whom to cling
if your nerves are done in
by a beach-bird's soft din
which it makes every time that it praises the
    spring.

PREGNANCY SCANNING AT MEIRI-TUNGA IN RANGÁRVELLIR, 10 FEBRUARY

Þórdís, the farmer here, has two hundred and fifty sheep. She always has an unusually large number of three-lambed ewes: her flock is extremely fertile. Six people assist with the scanning – four of them women, which is an unusually high ratio. Farm folk commonly gather to help each other out when the pregnancy scanner comes. The success of my job also depends a lot on this support. It's wonderful to see the kids' interest in it: there's often a bunch of them gathered around the cage.

The scanning has to be done when the foetuses are a certain size. That imposes a very tight time schedule on the scanning season. If the foetuses are still too small or have grown too big, you can't easily see how many there are.

It can take a bit of practice to position the sensor in the right place on the groin, where there's no hair . . . and then to move it about . . . and it takes training to learn to read the results on the screen. This can be complicated, because the foetuses are swimming there in the uterus, turning about. It's the skeleton, the calcium, which appears on the screen. Preferably, I need to see as much as I can of the lamb: how it's positioned, its head and body, to ensure that I'm not seeing the same lamb from two different points of view and thinking that there are two – and vice versa. The main trick is to position the sensor in such a way as to get good images of the lambs and confirm whether there are one, two or three. It's much better not to struggle a lot doing this, as I did at the beginning; it was really tiring.

In pregnancy scanning, you have to be prepared for all sorts of situations. The sensor can malfunction or break, in which case it has to be sent back to Scotland for repair, which can cost up to half a million krónur. I have to have an extra sensor with me. And you really have to take care of the ultrasound reader, which can also malfunction.

More often, though, the cages or stools break because so much strain is put on them. These have been re-welded on so many farms, so much so that most farmers have welding equipment; and if not, the next farm over usually does.

It doesn't make things any easier that the sheep have to be a bit hungry. It makes them considerably more difficult to deal with than if they were fully fed and happy.

Pregnancy scanning is terribly hard on the body; having to sit there hunkered down in a cold sheephouse, repeating the same movement over and over with the sensor. Nor does it help that my hands get cold so easily. I have to keep a huge mitten collection in the car.

Lukewarm water in a tank next to me is pumped through the sensor to create conductivity through the skin. I have to wear foolproof rain trousers all the time, or I start getting soggy underneath, as I have the wet sensor over me. If it drips onto the stool and your pants aren't watertight, you're stuck with a wet bum . . . in a cold sheep-house for a whole day. It can get very uncomfortable, but like everything, you get used to it.

Underneath, I wear knitted underclothes from top to bottom. There was an emergency situation in that department around New Year when I discovered holes in all my socks and mittens; Mum was gone and unable to mend them. Things were looking pretty bad, but luckily for me, as soon as Mum started feeling better she asked for her knitting needles. I immediately grabbed her knitting bag and rushed to Hveragerði. Mum knitted and knitted, remedying the situation; and now I have new supplies of woollen clothing.

DEPO-PROVERA

In the autumn of 2008, I began feeling odd. My whole body ached and I was constantly tired. My condition continued to worsen for more than two years, until the end of January 2011. By then, things had become so bad that it felt like there was little left to do but shoot myself, which I most likely would have done had Ásta not suggested that I go and see Elísabet Reynisdóttir, a nutritional therapist.

At the start of that period, I was in a relationship that went all to pot – and with it the theory that love could conquer all – but that's another story. In that particular attempt at being in a relationship, I got the brilliant idea of using a contraceptive named Depo-Provera, which is injected intramuscularly once every three months. True to my habit of never reading instructions, I ignored the patient information label and everything else, and had the stuff pumped into me for over two years.

During that period I often went to see doctors, and they diagnosed me with fibromyalgia and osteoarthritis and prescribed all kinds of anti-rheumatics, nerve drugs and painkillers. I was on so many medications that I even had a discount card for them; but they had no effect.

I tried all kinds of things to get a grip on the situation. I stopped eating sugar and cut back on flour and coffee and my food intake in general. I didn't touch alcohol or snuff. Still, the situation didn't improve at all. I'm 1.81 metres tall and my weight dropped to 63 kilos – I was like a skeleton.

I thought it was my fault, and that all my shearing work and drudgery over the years had wrecked my body. I struggled my way through the days, went to bed at seven in the evening and slept for twelve hours. I really had to push myself to keep going; the muscles in my legs and arms kept giving out; the sheep slipped from my hands; soon even holding onto the handlebars of my quad bike became torturous, and I had no energy for anything other than trying to lurch through each day. I was dangerously anaemic, got urinary-tract infections for the first and last time in my life – so far, anyway – and had an irregular heartbeat and a 'sunken breastbone', whatever that means.

In the first months, I had blue shadows under my eyes, which later became permanent red bags, both under and at the corners of my eyes. I spent two pregnancy-scanning seasons like this. I dragged myself through them, and Ella worked twice as hard to cover for me. It shattered my self-confidence. I who had always been so big and strong, embracing all physical challenges, was suddenly uncertain if I could get things done.

I quit professional shearing, quit the police, didn't

go to the Workers' Weekend festival or to the round-up dances, or anywhere else where people were gathered, for that matter, unless I really had to. Then in January 2011, I finally went to see Beta, the nutritional therapist. She'd only been interviewing me for a quarter of an hour before she figured out what the problem was. Those huge doses of hormones were literally killing me.

Since then, Ásta – who would definitely have realized this immediately had I been in the habit of discussing contraception with her or anyone other than people in the health industry – has regularly pointed out all kinds of horror stories in connection with this drug. When Ásta and I took a look together at the side effects of Depo-Provera, we found that I'd experienced most of them: anaemia, urinary-tract infections, extreme fatigue and depression.

Naturally, I didn't take any more injections; I threw the medication out and drank chamomile tea until I got through the withdrawal symptoms from the nerve drugs that made me wake up trembling at night, firmly convinced that I was about to die – and then I started a pregnancy-scanning tour. By March, the red bags under my eyes were gone and I'd begun smiling again. By July, I was hiking in Hornstrandir with Fanney and Siggeir. I carried all our food, and ate most of it, too.

A year later, I was back up to full strength, and there's absolutely nothing wrong with me now except for my old prolapsed disc and the occasional back pain that it causes. The entire experience has taught me always to be grateful for waking up every morning as fit as a fiddle. Health and stamina are absolutely invaluable treasures.

The other day, I realized that those Depo-Provera years of mine are a bit of a haze; that I really can't remember them very well. I can usually recall fun times in minute detail. My memories of that time are so murky that I had to ask Fanney about a ten-day trip on horse back that we took in 2009, because I can barely remember whether we stayed in huts or a tent. I also usually remember all my work projects in detail. But I can barely remember the fence work, cultivation and other jobs during those years. I can only remember what a struggle it all was.

I wanted to tell this story in case it might help another woman out there who's inexplicably getting weaker and weaker and literally pleading tearfully with doctors, who only give her more medication and brochures about fibromyalgia.

HEIÐA THE EWE-PREGNANCY SCANNER ON FACEBOOK, 24 FEBRUARY 2016

'Looks like you're going to be doing some serious mopping!' said the girl at the cash register in the Bónus supermarket in Egilsstaðir, looking at the two large cans of Ajax in front of her. She was obviously polite – after all she wasn't suggesting that this foul-smelling pregnancy scanner should buy two bottles of shower gel instead and use them right away, or looking askance at the eight chocolate bars sharing the conveyor belt with the Ajax cans. Now it's three weeks later and soon my old Lux and I will be rolling into the farmyard at Sölvabakki in Eastern Húnavatn District, to meet up with the farmers and Logi. I'm so looking forward to it.

EVENING, 3 MARCH

I'm in Mjóifjörður in Ísafjarðardjúp, and due to reach my destination in Súgandafjörður around ten-ish. I caught a very bad cold along the way and now have almost no voice. Which, of course, isn't very convenient. The people in the sheep-house can barely hear me. They have to bend almost all the way down to do so. Only squeaky sounds come out when I try to say one of these: One! Two! Three!

I had such a high fever this morning that I thought I wouldn't make it through the day. Someone went to the pharmacy in Hólmavík to get me some Panodil Hot, so I've been drinking that every coffee break. It reduces my fever and relieves the pain.

I got this horrid cold in Húnavatn District ... of course. When there, I'd been boasting about always being healthy as an ox and never coming down with anything. But working on such good farms in Strandir has helped me so much in this illness. These are dream places, all their organization exemplary; everything is carried for me, the cage taken off my hands and the sonar as well. And they run around shutting all the windows because of the state I'm in. On one of the farms they even nailed over a hole in the wall so that the breeze wouldn't blow in to bother the sick pregnancy scanner.

One day at a farm in Strandir, my colleague Logi started throwing up in the farmyard. Afterwards, he was fine. I'm not sure the Strandir people really want us back . . . we're nothing better than plague rats. Thank goodness the weather is fine now, good road conditions, just small icy patches. The weather being so kind has helped us immensely on this tour.

FOUR ANECDOTES ABOUT ELLA AND HEIÐA DOING PREGNANCY SCANNING

Delicate movements become difficult after long days clutching a ridiculously expensive sensor with all your might. Once we were having afternoon coffee with Ármann and Jóna at their wonderful farm named Dalir, out east in Fáskrúðsfjörður. On the table was a delicious-looking cake, and I reached for the knife to cut a piece for myself. Inadvertently, I gripped it as tightly as I do the sensor, and the knife whisked through the cake and flung the piece out onto the floor. Luckily, the plate was made of strong material, because it survived the attack. I do try not to behave like a barbarian at other people's farms, so I was utterly mortified, but those fine folk acted as if flying pieces of cake were nothing out of the ordinary. To make matters worse, two years earlier Ella tripped and fell down the front steps at Dalir, so it would be fair to say that the two of us have made better impressions elsewhere than at this particular farm.

One evening we were driving to Hólmavík and stopped to grab some coffee and chocolate at Hamraborg, which is the best shop in Ísafjörður, in our opinion. I was the first one back out to the car and had already taken my seat when Ella came hurrying out, coffee cup in hand as usual. She was wearing her rubber shoes, of course, and the parking lot was covered with smooth ice. She stormed in front of the car and suddenly disappeared. A second later, a sturdy hand slammed onto the hood of my old Lux and up sprang Ella, coffee cup still in hand. She continued on her way to the passenger door and got in the car. I sensed her seriousness and asked immediately: 'Did you spill your coffee?' 'Not a drop,' said Ella. Only then was it safe to burst out laughing – and we sped off towards Strandir.

The two of us are highly coordinated and have become quick at cleaning and packing up our gear after scanning. Only once has this coordination gone wrong, and that was in the sheep-house at the farm of my cousins Jónas and Ísleifur, at Kálfholt in Ásar Municipality. Ella grabbed the stool and strode away with it just as I was going to sit down on it to unhook the machine. I ended up on my back there in the narrow run in the sheep-house. Ella, startled by the commotion, turned round and burst out laughing – and didn't really stop until much later in the day.

The farm where we scan the greatest number of sheep, twelve to thirteen hundred of them, is Uppsalir, in Eastern Húnavatn District. We and the assisting crew are well looked after there. One year, as so often before, they'd prepared a coffee buffet by laying a board over the feeder aisle in the sheep-house and loading it with coffee cups and the coffeepot, containers of sandwiches, baked goods and other such things. Ella was scanning and I was hanging out in the feeder aisle. When one of the sheep got out of the cage, as often happens, I focused all my attention on making sure that the right sheep was caught. In all the commotion, I made the very bad decision of jumping up onto the feeder rail to get a better look – I lost my balance and stepped with all my weight onto the buffet board, which immediately sprang from its place, causing everything on it to abandon the party and the glass inside the coffeepot to shatter into a thousand pieces. They're hardly the best guests at a tea party, these pregnancy scanners.

NINE IN THE EVENING, 8 MARCH

Now I'm on Steingrímsfjörður Heath. The road conditions are excellent and the weather is perfect. I'm taking the new road, Þröskuldar, from Strandir over to Reykhólasveit. I'd been scanning at Svansvík in the eastern part of Ísafjarðardjúp, and finished at a quarter past seven. Then I went and had something to eat. I'm not really tired now. But this cold-and-fever thing has been really wearying. Pregnancy scanning requires concentration, which doesn't mix well with illness. Luckily, all the farms where I was staying were good places to be ill.

The farmers here in the Westfjords, especially the women, throw safety nets around me. They call ahead to the next farm where I'm expected and ask: 'Has she arrived yet?' On this particular leg of the tour, my benefactor, that genius Guðmundur from Bassastaðir in Strandir, sometimes called Brandur Bassi, phoned the farm I was expected at and said: 'I think she might not make it this time. I think she has such a bad cold that she'll die.'

I'm fine now, apart from the persistent cough. The fever's gone and I'm back at full strength. I was with my colleague Logi the last few days. Now he's going home to Borgarfjörður to see his wife and little daughter. Then he'll come out again with me tomorrow morning to do the scanning in Árnes District. We'll stay with Fanney in Hveragerði. I should arrive at her place around midnight.

Ten o'clock in the evening

Now I'm heading down Þröskuldar. I should be in Hveragerði around one-ish. I got up at seven this morning, as usual, so this is turning out to be a long day.

I so look forward to seeing my Fífill. I'm sure he'll wake up when I arrive; German Shepherds are guard dogs, after all, and that instinct was noticeably strong in him even as puppy. It was terrible to leave him behind when I went off to do my scanning. It's been six whole weeks.

I'm planning on treating myself a bit. I've always loved playing on the snowmobile. But after Christmas, I was so tired and depressed from all the trouble with the Búland Power Plant that I could barely look at it. It was the registered letters that stressed me out the most. There was also a very difficult town meeting in Klaustur, which caused me a great deal of distress.

But I couldn't bear letting those power-plant men defeat me like that. It was such a relief finally to hire a lawyer to back me up in the fight. And so when I saw an advertisement for snowmobile tours in Strandir, I made a reservation. After Easter, I'll throw the sledge onto a trailer and head up there. It's a guided tour, and we'll be staying in Djúpavík. It'll be good to do something like this with other people. I usually go snowmobiling alone. And it isn't a very clever idea to be traipsing around the mountains on a snowmobile by yourself.

As previously mentioned, I'm a petrolhead. I get an adrenaline kick from the smell of a two-stroke engine and I usually really like the smell of petrol and oil. And there's something so exciting about hearing the roar of the engine of a quad bike or snowmobile.

HEIÐA AT A POETRY MEET-UP

I sometimes wondered, looking at Facebook, if it's I who am such a huge failure or if everyone is just weird. There are so many people there who pour out their hearts and love for their better halves. You know, all the photos and 'it's my darling's birthday today' . . . 'out for dinner with my sweetheart' . . . 'my sweetie out walking the dog', and so forth.

I never found the need for this sort of expression until this powerful, perky fellow came into my life at the end of 2011. I feel so good when I'm with him, and my most fun moments are when we go roaming around the mountains together, and yes, I have to admit that I've not only put pictures of him but also posted mushy status updates on Facebook. He's just so wonderful.

You sing with such power and verve in my ear.
With gladness you fill me; I'm thrilled that you're
    mine.
No sweeter snowmobile than you, oh my dear,
My Polaris 600, so fine.

SHEARING COMPETITIONS

In some respects, I regret ending my professional shearing career, despite it being such hard work, even harder than pregnancy scanning. It's especially hard on your shoulders and back, but I've always been involved in physically demanding work. If that hadn't been the case, I would have probably spent loads of time at the gym. Or else not – and ended up tipping the scales at two hundred kilograms. It's really fun to compete in shearing, which is something I've been dabbling in now in my old age, something that I didn't do when it was my job. Now shearing has become my main hobby.

The thing that frightens me is getting stuck. I'm constantly on the lookout for new challenges. To try something, do something different. When you no longer want to take on new projects on a farm, you should quit.

I've been taking courses abroad in order to learn how to shear properly – not just rip the wool off fast enough and get paid, as it was for the most part in the professional business. It's so much fun when you feel like you've mastered the techniques of shearing, when you can handle both the shears and the sheep properly. It's a blast, in fact. So much so that now, shortly after New Year, I'll be going to New Zealand to take part in the 2017 World Championships.

In Iceland, only men tend to compete in shearing, and I'll be the only woman from Iceland taking part in this competition. Of course, many women here know how to shear, but they haven't had the chance to compete. On the other hand, it's pretty common to see women doing this in other countries. Emily Welch, for instance, is a world record holder, and an amazing shearer. In New Zealand there are a lot of women who shear, and their number is growing. They're in mixed shearing teams, and there are also teams composed solely of women.

I'm so looking forward to going to New Zealand. It's been a dream of mine for twenty years. I can't imagine anything other than all Icelandic farmers wanting to see that sheep mecca, New Zealand.

My colleague Hafliði and I will be gone for five whole weeks. First, we'll do shearing in New Zealand. They've got farmers there to take in crazy foreigners like us. We'll be part of a team given instruction and training. We'll not only be provided with housing and food, but we'll be paid, too, so that will help somewhat with our travel costs.

Hafliði's wife, Guðný Gréta, and her sister Halla will come later, and then we'll tour around a bit together. I'll be doing the driving, seeing as how everyone lived to tell the tale after driving around with me on the left-hand side of the road in Britain.

One of my fondest memories from the shearing competition in Yorkshire was watching the New Zealander Sir David Fagan, who's a legend in the shearing business. He's getting older now, but had to come with his son, and competed in the same group with him.

It's no joke leaving the farm for six weeks, as I do during pregnancy scanning. I have so many responsibilities, which makes it hard to leave. It's tough not being there to keep things running and look after the flock. And it's hard to leave Mum. I know that the terrible weather and storms at this time of year frighten her, and I feel bad not being with her. But her sister Þóra often comes when I'm not there. She was there the whole six weeks I was away, because Mum's leg is still so bad.

Once I get back, there's so much work to catch up on. I dive straight into hoof trimming, as the hooves of these well-fed sheep grow excessively. For this I use a specially designed stall. It's so much easier than having to flip the sheep onto their backsides. But this is one of those jobs that you can't do on your own, no matter how strong and agile you are. Both Fanney and Siggeir have helped me. It's a two-and-a-half-day job, turning a whole herd upside down in a stall.

Then after hoof trimming, I do the winter wool cropping, which takes another two and a half days. And then comes the crash – which can actually be overwhelming. I sometimes feel like my exhaustion is going to kill me. I feel so ill. So I sleep and sleep in my recliner, and can only just about manage the feeding. And really – just don't talk to me.

This paralysis lasts for a few days. Then I start scraping myself back together. The exhaustion is both physical and mental. I sometimes feel as if a ten-wheeler lorry just ran me over.

I tried to prepare Logi for the let-down, warned him that he'd feel like hell. And I don't think he believed me. But then he told me after the depression had passed: 'Now I understand what you're talking about. I was wiped out.'

Once I feel better, I start preparing for lambing. April always goes by very quickly. Around mid-April, I start repairing the fences. That job needs to be finished before lambing, which starts at the end of April or beginning of May, and kicks into full gear around 10 May. I have long fences that get badly damaged over the winter, when the snow can be so heavy.

In the spring of 2014, Þór Saari started coming voluntarily to help fix the fences. Others had talked about coming to help me, since I needed to take time that I didn't really have in order to fight Suðurorka and do my council work. Which, ultimately, wasn't a private matter but rather a kind of civil obligation. In the end, Þór Saari was the only volunteer who came to help; and I never chased down the other promised support. But Þór was determined to keep his word, contacting me steadfastly and asking about jobs that needed doing. Now he's my permanent fence master. He's a great guy, an extremely easy-going team player. He works flat out, and is usually pretty tired when he comes to the house to gulp down milk and biscuits during breaks.

The snowmobile tour was fantastic. It was fine being the only woman on it. With so many experienced snow-mobilers and guides, I was in good hands. I learned a lot, and enjoyed my snowmobile and myself more than I've ever done rattling around here at home. These were cheerful, lively men who liked to tell stories, to talk about snowmobiles and outdoor activities. There wasn't a single word about agricultural product agree-ments, power plants or politics the entire weekend. I liked not having to talk too much, and I didn't neces-sarily feel the need to take part in conversations. I didn't have to put on the kind of show I sometimes feel forced to. It's nice not needing to be the centre of attention. You also notice all sorts of things that you might have missed, otherwise.

SPRING

HEIÐA AT A POETRY MEET-UP

People often feel sorry for me for being alone, and I often feel sorry for people for living with others. One autumn several years ago, a few men in the district became downright enraged with each other during the round-up. I don't know how it all started as I was herding in a different place, but I witnessed how, at the end of the day, they tore off, furious as hell, from the old milk-can platform where the fight had taken place, quad bikes and cars peeling out in every direction and against all traffic laws, dogs running for their lives, gravel flying as if it would never land and black smoke filling the sky. As I slowly drove my old Lux home, my quad in its bed, I started thinking what fun it would be for their wives when the men came home and began telling them about their day:

These men's behaviour goes way overboard,
peeling out, spitting gravel, and such.
I simply say nothing and thank the good Lord
that I'm still on my own – they're too much!

CYCLES

At the approach of spring, the sheep become intolerable. They get frustrated about being inside and act restless. It starts getting better around mid-May, once you can begin letting them out of the sheep-houses in groups during lambing.

The farmer's job is an endless cycle. At the same time, there's a lot of variety within it. It's wonderful to meet your sheep again in the autumn, particularly a few old friends, such as Svakaspaka (Super Wise) and the sisters Stika (Stride) and Systa (Sis). It's just as wonderful to let them out of the sheep-houses during lambing, then onto the hayfields and finally, in groups, out of your sight completely, up onto the heaths.

The farmer's job also involves great preparation. The whole summer is actually just preparation for the next winter. You have to make and put up supplies of hay, prepare the houses for the winter, do all the necessary maintenance work on them to ensure that they're storm- and blizzard-proof. Siggeir is my mainstay in this, as in so many other things. He and I work together to maintain the walls of the turf houses.

Preparation for winter also includes storing all the machinery, equipment, tools and building materials, such as fencing material and timber. It all needs to be locked up good and tight. I tie and nail shut the old lamb house, and then ask God to bless it. Following winter storms, I peek between my fingers to see if it's still there.

Time goes by so quickly that I feel as if I pretty much make one ring around the Christmas tree, and then it's spring again. Spring and the beginning of summer are all about getting everything out: sheep, hens, haymaking equipment, the goat. And then there are the 'homestayers', which is what the people of Skaftafell call bottle lambs.

Throughout the month of April, I get seriously preoccupied thinking about lambing, and it's so much fun when the first lamb is born. But you've had your complete fill of it by the time it's over.

It's fun to start the haymaking, and likewise such a relief when it's finished. And sheer bliss when it all goes well. No matter what job it is. I enjoy it when there's a lot going on and I'm busiest. That's when I feel best.

ONE-PERSON JOBS

Once on a pregnancy-scanning tour, Ella and I listened to an experienced farmer talking about the various jobs that were impossible to do alone. He picked out dehorning a ram as the prime example. We bit our tongues, as both of us had often done that job on our own.

I do admit that I sweated so much with the effort that there wasn't a dry thread left on me by the end of it. But you have to dehorn rams when their horns start growing directly towards their faces, as they would grow into their heads if nothing were done. At worst, it can be painful for the animal when the tips of its horns are sawn off. Nowadays it's forbidden to dehorn rams without the assistance of a vet, and then you can only do it if the ram is sedated. Luckily, this isn't a very common problem.

In general, I've learned to trust myself first and foremost in most jobs. I'm not in a position to call for help whenever I need it, and I try to avoid doing so as much as possible. You simply learn to assess the circumstances, determine what you can get done on your own and try to think of different ways of doing things, especially with those jobs that might appear at first glance to be impossible to manage.

My quad bike is essential. It enables me to round up sheep on my own across large areas, which wouldn't be possible on foot or horseback. My sheep have learned to obey the quad too; when they hear it, they know that the game is up, and they get moving in the right direction.

Now the sheep give me attitude if I try to herd them into the corral on foot. They just scatter all around me. Even with more people to help, that hasn't always worked – but once the sheep hear the quad, they put on grumpy faces and run to wherever it is they're supposed to go.

FIVE HUNDRED SHEEP
AND ONE GOAT

My goat, Leiknir (Dextrous), was a Christmas present to me from five friends. He's huge and has very big horns. He's also a boisterous creature who takes up a lot of space and wants to have the entire feeder to himself. But goats don't eat or drink much, and are in that sense very cost-efficient.

Leiknir does as I say, and shrinks if I scold him. I have yet to come across a ram that behaves like that. Goats are much more like dogs when it comes to temperament. Sheep are so stubborn that they do the exact opposite of what they're supposed to do unless, of course, they're purebred leader sheep that will hold completely still when you're shearing them and wait patiently for it to be finished.

When you hold a goat kid, it's completely relaxed, but with lambs there's always some tension. Kids are among the most loveable animals I can think of.

Leiknir goes with the sheep to the mountains and is herded back down with them in the autumn. My neighbour Jói was working on his pasture fence last summer when he caught sight of that huge goat of mine up on the cliffs, and thought he had lost his mind.

I've only got round to naming about a hundred of my five hundred sheep, including Svakaspaka (Super Wise), Sírena (Siren), Sálfræði (Psychology), Áskorun (Challenge), Árátta (Fixation). Sjónskerta Mora (Visually-Impaired Russet) is a favourite; she's calm and fun.

Then there are the pairs of sisters, Æra (Honour) and Væra (Peaceful), and Gulrót (Carrot) and Rófa (Swede). The brother and sister Laukur (Onion) and Paprika (Bell Pepper) are still alive. One of the sheep was named Sperrirófa (Show-off). She belonged to Adda, who used a dictionary to pinpoint the perfect name. Everyone really missed that sheep after she was gone.

It's undeniable that sheep farming means constant drudgery and bother, for small financial gain. Still, you can't just leave it at that. There are so many other factors that have to be taken into account. I live in a big house with a huge garden that stretches over more than six thousand hectares. My mum and I are the only two in that entire area. How many people would there be packed into six thousand hectares in other parts of the world?

In Reykjavik, it costs ninety thousand krónur per month to rent a room with access to a kitchen. The people in Reykjavik aren't working any less, and the rental market there is insane. And then you could get pushed out of your rented apartment, without being able to afford to buy your own. There are all sorts of privileges that come with being a farmer. If you're like me, a petrolhead with a weakness for snowmobiles and an obsession with quad bikes, then you don't need a trailer to transport them to a place where you can play on them. You can just start the engine and drive off. Another privilege is in knowing exactly where the good, healthy food that you're eating comes from. And you're completely dependent on yourself too. That's priceless.

A good farmer has to be resourceful. You have to tackle whatever difficulties the weather and the forces of nature throw at you. Each year is different. Some years, the farming can be more difficult because of winterkill and dampness. Or the hay goes bad. Or you have trouble with the lambs. Last year, we had to keep feeding the sheep hay well into the summer. Feeding hay is not only a lot of work; it can be very expensive too. Bookkeeping in this business can be tough to keep straight sometimes.

THE BRIGHT FARM

The teacher and writer Stefán Hannesson was a child at
Ljótarstaðir, living there until he was twelve. He wrote
a beautiful poem, 'Ljótarstaðir': a vivid testament to the
life cycle of farming, which in my view must persist,
here as elsewhere. From one sheep to the next and from
one man to the next. The poem opens with his address-
ing the farm:

Ljótarstaðir, long it's been
since I within your pastures played.
Green to pale, snow-covered, then
the fields thawed, and hay was made.
My mind holds wondrous pictures of
the lively springs; nights starry, still,
and cloudless summer skies above
Austurtún and Enni hill.

Moldir, Hóll and Stakkatún
all lovely; as was drifted snow
on Sýrdalshraun and Fjalldalsbrún –
my memories with light do glow.

Though work there was no child's game –
day after day, and at times night,
through every season – all the same;
yet in this, too – we took delight.

When Stefán wrote the poem, Ljótarstaðir had been
abandoned for several years, until my grandfather and
grandmother moved here with my dad and his siblings,
in 1952.

One line in the poem reads:

No voices on my bright farm now . . .

Here he picks out precisely the same meaning that the
farm's name, Ljótarstaðir, has for me: the bright farm.

PEOPLE, AND
JUDGING CHARACTER

I don't know if I'm a good judge of character. I've certainly made mistakes, and been burned because of it. If I like someone, I like that person through thick and thin. But if someone crosses the line with me, then that's it, and there's no way back from there.

There are some people I would have been happy to get to know better, but never got the chance. I'm not good at pursuing things like that, and am also bad at keeping in touch. If you don't return their visits and calls, people give up on you, and in the end they stop coming. This, of course, is a disadvantage in the sense that your network of connections shrinks; you don't have as many friends as you could have had to talk to and make plans and have fun with when you have the time. Whenever that is!

Then of course there are some I wouldn't even give the time of day to . . . but mostly I try to take people as they are. I have no time for people who are narrow-minded. I can't bear prejudice based on skin colour, race, sexual orientation, nationality. I can't bear violence against humans and animals. I can't bear judging and backbiting. And I imagine that those who speak badly about everything and everyone probably don't speak any more kindly about me.

I have a strong sense of the gap between Reykjavik and these remote rural areas. People out here mock the people in Reykjavik as idiots who can't even drive in the snow. But they forget that those in Reykjavik may have other sensibilities that we in the rural areas lack.

MENTAL EXTRAVAGANCE

Most folks have it quite the same,
with little variation:
meeting, kissing, goes the game;
then bed for jubilation.

I have no clue when it comes to what men think of me,
whether they find me attractive or not. To be honest, I
don't give it a second thought; don't notice it unless I'm
told directly. I'm not on my own because I've been
sitting crying into a handkerchief or an apron over a
lack of interested men. I've been made every offer
imaginable over the years. Men offer themselves, their
sons . . . drunk fathers sometimes call me up and say
things like 'Do you need a farmhand?' or 'I can lift the
hay bales' or 'I can repair your tractors'. Sometimes
they send letters, jewellery and all sorts of other things.

My favourite example, though, was when an uncle of
mine sent a man to court me. Knowing his niece, he
didn't send the fellow with gifts of flowers and
chocolates, but with a hammer and jump leads. I didn't
realize until much later that he was actually interested

in me. I just thanked him for his gifts, went and got Dad and left him to chat with the visitor while I went off to do my work.

I do realize that men can feel threatened: some have said, 'You're so independent.' I've received lots of unsolicited advice: been told I should be more yielding, look at them with submissive, Bambi-like eyes – and definitely not act in such an independent way because it can be undermining and make men feel inferior and, you know, I'll never get a man like that. Because that, after all, is my only purpose in life – oh, absolutely!

Apart from the independence problem, I'm tall and there's such a strong tradition that the man should be the taller one. There's simply no end to adversity in this world!

If men feel threatened by me I really couldn't care less; it's their problem. Maybe I've become so thick-skinned now that nothing can get through.

I once heard a definition of 'romantic' that I really liked. It apparently comes from the Eastfjords: mental extravagance.

I often say, both jokingly and seriously, that I'm as romantic as a block of frozen cod.

Matters of the heart aren't a priority for me, and I'm very wary of commitment. I know that's not normal. Even when I was at school, I couldn't help noticing that most of the other girls thought far more about marriage and childbearing than I did. My priorities were always different: my focus on what sort of work I wanted to do; where I wanted to live; and what I wanted to accomplish.

At the same time, I know that family life can be fantastic, as I can see it is for my friend Linda. In a certain way, it keeps me connected to reality to witness how happy her family is, and how great her kids are. There is, of course, such a thing as good, traditional family life, and I'm well aware that people successfully live their lives differently than I do. But I also remember thinking, when I was little: why does life have to be so sad when you're an adult? I found it so strange that life was supposed to fit into a specific framework. Maybe it was the attitude here at home that adults shouldn't be gallivanting around, following whims.

I was repeatedly told when I was little that I could start farming once I'd found a husband. But why should I need a husband? And why did I have to have a husband in order to start farming? It was also assumed that I would have children. I didn't get it and I still don't.

But kids seem naturally drawn to me. The pupils that I was responsible for in Kirkjubæjarklaustur, as both their physical education teacher and class mentor, were loads of fun and I had a blast with them. They liked me so much that I usually had three or four of the rug rats hanging off me whenever we went for walks or played outside. I was younger than the other teachers and enjoyed goofing around with the kids. The bigger boys sometimes formed a line in the hallway, blocking it, until I had to break through their line. But there was no lack of discipline; they obeyed me whenever they needed to.

19 APRIL

I had a gut feeling this morning that something bad was coming. I was most afraid that a sheep was going to get sick. But it was Ólafur Ragnar Grímsson, our president, announcing that he was standing for election again. It's awful when people don't know when to stop, like the old farmers who cling onto their farms and make it very difficult for the younger generation to take over.

AT LJÓTARSTAÐIR IN
MAY – LAMBING

Lambing can sometimes turn into a kind of third-rate horror movie. But it's usually a fascinating time. The farmer becomes both midwife and obstetrician. You have to work as carefully as possible under a great deal of stress. And it can often become quite gruesome.

Money is always tight in sheep farming and if a sheep can't give birth, some farmers resort to shooting it. I can't bear the thought of doing this, so I get the vet to come out and perform a Caesarean, which is very expensive. But it's worth it if the lamb comes out alive, and then the sheep goes on to bear more healthy lambs.

Lars Hansen, our vet, did two C-sections for me last year. We set up an operating table and put the sheep to sleep. The area to be operated on is shaved and sanitized, and the uterus is cut open. I'm always there watching attentively. I'm not squeamish.

The ewes are such perfect animals. Their wombs contract in no time. They're so incredibly quick to pop their cervixes back that it all needs to be sewn up in a flash – the uterus and then the two abdominal layers are speedily sutured shut. Later, the sutures dissolve, but at first the seams bulge, like the ties on a liverwurst. But by the time you do the shearing in the autumn, you can't see any scars or other signs of the operation.

After the procedure, the ewe is given painkillers and penicillin to prevent infection. Then she wakes up and starts feeding and taking care of her lamb. I've never had any trouble with a sheep after a C-section.

Lambing takes several weeks. I spread out the workload deliberately, but on many farms the rams are put in with the all the ewes at the same time. My lambing lasts from 27 April until the end of May, and reaches its peak 10–17 May. It would be impossible on my own. Fanney usually comes and stays to help out, and she takes the night shift. Her daughter María Ösp has come here for lambing since she was little, and has become very skilled in its tricks. This spring, she'll be here the whole time. Back in the day, my Aunt Birna always took a week off work and stayed with us for ten days during the peak time.

The spring of 2015 was a very difficult one; it stayed cold and snowy well into May. Many of the ewes had to remain inside into June, and be fed hay, which meant a lot of extra work and cost. For health reasons, the sheep must be kept dry or there's an increased risk of uterine inflammations and other disorders. During lambing, the sheep-house floors need to be strewn with clean, dry straw. That spring, I used fourteen bales of straw. The straw is expensive; this is all very costly. So it was a difficult time, but the excellent summer that came in its wake more than made up for it. Such a terrible season forces me into a sense of gratitude for easier times for several years afterwards. It's good to have something to bring you back down to earth. Springs like that come round more often than anyone likes. But we're quick to forget the bad times.

Giving birth is harder for the ewes than it used to be, because the lambs are so big now and the ewes aren't in quite as good shape because they lie inside all winter, overeating and grunting. It's pretty common these days for the lambs to be turned in the wrong direction, or for multiple lambs to be all tangled up, and for these and all kind of other reasons a lot of ewes can need help with delivery.

I use forceps quite often, and sometimes a lambing snare. It isn't a very complicated tool, just a pipe with a plastic-coated string running through it. But I use it to help every day. This is because the unborn lambs can have big horns, especially the rams. You hook the snare behind the horns to help pull the lamb out so that it takes less time for the ewe to deliver, which proves much more comfortable for both the ewe and the lamb. I always help speed up the process rather than let them strain in labour for a longer time.

But there's a definite art to it. You can't be too hasty – can't start helping before a ewe is ready and has opened up. You have to give them time; this is something you learn.

When a ewe is about to give birth, you start by checking whether the lamb is in the right position. If not, you intervene earlier.

While I'm helping a ewe, I talk to her constantly, telling her to be calm, and that everything is going to be all right. This helps to calm both of us. María has adopted this habit from me. But this isn't too out of the ordinary: I think it's quite common for farmers to talk a lot to their animals.

A good farmer always needs to make sure that the ewes are well-balanced, but especially during lambing. If they become stressed, they start knocking either each other or other ewes' lambs about, or even worse, reject their own lambs.

In March this year, I advertised on Facebook for a female lambing assistant:

A lambing assistant urgently needed for all of May or the first part of May. The job will involve helping deliver lambs during the afternoons and the night, until the birds start to stir around 04:00. Experience with farm work is preferable, kindness towards animals, strict work habits and tidiness required. Stamina, motivation and cheerfulness necessary.

Sandra is coming to help; she has a degree in agriculture and experience in lambing, and is going to stay here for a month with María and me.

Our livelihood depends on lambing. You've got to have good hay, and enough of it. If we ensure that the ewes and lambs get a good start in life, they'll be in excellent shape when they come down from the mountains in the autumn. Farming is more than just a normal business because it's a livelihood based on the welfare of living creatures. It's hard to think of the animals suffering from a storm or fire, or accidents.

This April, one of the sheep got stuck on her back in the sheep-house. Even inside, this can prove fatal, because they can't last lying in that position for very long. Usually they suffocate, because their stomachs slip forward and press against the organs in their chest cavity. By the time we got to her, this particular sheep was still alive, but because she couldn't get up other sheep had trampled her and she'd been injured. There was nothing else to do but get the gun.

Sheep should only lie down for short periods of time to avoid pressure sores. This can lead to death, but you keep trying to save them, giving them doses of very expensive penicillin even if you know how it will end. You can hardly ever get a sheep to recover if it's been lying still for two or three days. All the same, you have to keep trying.

In the final weeks before lambing, you have to feed the ewes a lot of hay. Up until this time, the foetuses are still small as beans, but they start growing rapidly in the final few weeks. If the ewes don't get enough to eat during that time, they can quickly waste away. The ones with three lambs need the most; they're kept separate from the others. During this time, I go through three bales of hay per day and during lambing, even more. I feed the sheep twice daily. Each round bale weighs around six hundred kilos and I have to move them using the tractor and pallet jacks.

It's taken a few months, but Fífill has got used to the sheep-houses. He's particularly fond of Svakaspaka. So much so that he nibbles at her horns and puts her head in his mouth. It's a pretty frightening sight, actually. But they're great friends.

I've never had so many people here helping me during lambing. There are three of us – María, Sandra and myself – and I feel spoiled. I really needed a good team to fill the very noticeable gap left by Mum's absence; she can't be out in the sheep-house any more, with her bad leg. In my first years here, Mum took the night shifts during lambing. Later, she worked with me a lot during the day, seeing to the feeding of the lambs herself.

We work in shifts. María and I get up at four in the morning and work until about eight in the evening. I try not to work after that, and to go to bed quickly. It's a luxury to be able to sleep for six hours straight at this time of year.

Sandra goes to work at about three or four in the afternoon, and comes back at about four in the morning. She can handle it herself when the sheep give birth, and doesn't need to wake me. Sandra came here by plane, as her dad is a pilot. They landed here in the hayfield, no less.

My sisters Stella and Fanney also came for five days during the peak. During lambing, there's no way that I can leave the farm unless Fanney is there to take control. She's done so the two times that I left for an entire day to speak at conferences in Reykjavik. I wouldn't allow anyone else to drop in like that and take over. Those who are familiar with lambing understand perfectly. There are so many things that can go wrong in a single day, both financially and emotionally. And I could never have left, as I did, without knowing that it would be all right.

My ewes can be aggressive towards strangers. Sandra has the bruises to show it. The ewes are much better to me and to María, who has spent so much time here. I was really worried about the assistant who was here last year because she was so small and slim. But it turned out okay in the end.

The sheep are in four different places inside, as well as out on the field, where you need to keep a keen eye on them. When we take hay bales to the sheep that are outside, we check on them.

Every once in a while during lambing, a sheep dies for no apparent reason. Yesterday, I found Pálína dead. I don't know what killed her. Her lambs were next to her, bleating loudly. They seemed to know what was going on, and jostled around me as I was burying her, which I did immediately. I couldn't use the usual tractor bucket because she'd died in a ravine. So I had to shovel by hand. I really hate the sight of dead animals, and always bury them quickly.

Pálína was white with a black head, black legs and black belly: she was a beautiful animal, and a great loss.

She always gave birth to such beautiful lambs too, with the same colour pattern. But without their mother, these lambs won't do well this summer, as they've grown too big for bottle-feeding. I just have to hope that they stick together and stay in the hayfields.

Lambing also means constantly shifting the sheep around – a game of constant moving and rearranging, making sure that there's always enough room for the ewes that have just given birth, as well as the ones with older lambs. I'll end up with around fourteen hundred sheep, so I have to organize things meticulously.

We keep them in stalls for four or five days after birth, two ewes and their lambs per stall. One of the jobs needing doing during lambing is earmarking all the lambs when they're moved out of the stalls. They're tagged during the first twenty-four hours. This is Sandra's job now. When she goes to the sheep-houses around afternoon coffee time, she tags all the lambs that have been born that day; and she gives each lamb its own number. This makes it easier to know where they belong in case they wander from their stalls.

It's crucial to be completely organized; to know where each sheep and each lamb in the flock is at any given time. When the lambs are between four and five days old, I move the ewes to a larger, shared space, usually with access to a large outdoor paddock. When it's time for them to leave there, the lot of them are given an anthelmintic (anti-parasitic drug) and then they're driven out to the hayfields. From there they go to the large fenced pastures, and finally up into the highland pastures.

There are so many things that need attention during lambing. You have to keep constant track of space, making sure that there's room enough for newborn lambs and their mothers to last the evening and night, for example. To move newly delivered ewes and their lambs to the stalls, you pick up the lambs and the mother follows. You just have to make sure that the mother can always see her lamb or lambs.

Once all the houses are full, the oldest lambs need to be released into the fields. And then the new batch moves into the space that's been emptied. It takes up a great amount of space when all of the ewes have given birth. The whole process requires a large amount of land.

One of the tasks that you can't really do on your own is loading up the sheep into the wagon before driving them out to the fields. There's a lot of hustle and bustle involved in this, and the right lambs have to remain with the right mothers. I move eight sheep and their lambs at a time. After releasing them into the field, I wait for a while and keep watch to make sure that nothing has gone wrong.

Then there's giving all the sheep the anthelmintic they need. By that time, the lambs are around five to ten kilos, depending on their age. I have to lift each one and administer the pills orally. I've never calculated how many kilograms in total I lift per hour in doing so. It's probably similar to the amount that those CrossFit girls lift with their kettlebells.

During this busy time, it's vital to prioritize well. When things start piling up, you have to decide what has to be done immediately and what can wait.

Taking care of the lambs is a huge job. You have to get to the lambs when they're newly born, before they start to suckle. Then you have to clean the ewes' teats and give the lambs a boost of colostrum, which is important for the development of their bodies' natural defences against disease. Then you should feed them probiotic yoghurt, to stimulate the formation of protective bacteria in their guts. During lambing when the humidity and heat increase in the sheep-houses, colibacillosis can strike: but giving the lambs an anti-diarrhoeal right after birth staves off this bacterial infection.

We write memos on a marker board, listing the lambs that need extra milk or the sheep that need injections. The stalls are numbered, so that you can go straight to the lamb or sheep needing attention. We write down everything because it's so incredibly easy to forget things and there are so many different things to think about. So when Sandra goes out to the sheep-houses, everything is written on the marker board for her, and she writes down what's needed before María and I take over.

In farming it's necessary to be vigilant in general, but during lambing you've got to ramp it up. You've got to inspect the different groups of sheep closely, listen for different sounds, such as a strange sound from a corner, where a ewe may have lain down on top of a lamb. And you've got to watch out for lambs whose mothers won't let them suckle.

If a lamb wanders away from its mother for some time, occasionally she pretends not to recognize it again. That really gets on my nerves. The sheep, in other words, can be pretty mean; we have an unusually large number of such cases now, particularly two-lambed ewes not wanting one of their lambs. You have to step in and help, and hope that you can sort things out. But this behaviour bothers me.

It's our fault if we mess up re-accustoming a lamb to its mother, or accustoming an orphan lamb to a new mother. Our fault if we don't notice early enough that something is wrong. But it can be difficult to accustom a second lamb to a single-lambed ewe, especially if it's an older ewe. They sometimes know perfectly well that they gave birth to just one lamb.

We have eleven bottle lambs at the moment. We've never had so many. They have to be fed every four hours. We also have ten other lambs whose suckling is being supplemented with bottle-feeding because they're not getting enough milk from their mothers.

Every evening and morning, hay feeding takes a long time because the sheep are in four places, two of which aren't right next to the farmhouse. We also have to put hay out on the fields. There's a lot of strain on the sheep during lambing. While they're milking, they need to be given first-class hay, grass that was cut while it was still growing. For ewes with two lambs, it's even more exhausting. They have to dip deep into their own reserves, regardless of how much hay they eat.

The lambs need to start grazing on grass or eating hay, and have access to water, at around a week old, and preferably sooner, or they take too much from the ewes. They're often still inside at two weeks old and learning to eat hay, which they'll then know how to do in the autumn. Back in the day, the sheep didn't stay inside for so long, which meant that the lambs didn't learn how to eat hay during springtime. Then it could be tricky teaching them how to do so in the autumn.

Once a day, we strew straw on the floors of the sheep-houses. Straw is what's left over from cutting grain – the stalks and bracts of the grain. It's lifeless; there's no nutrition in it. The straw is a key element in lambing, because it helps keep the sheep dry. Our straw was stored all winter and bundled in April, and is especially dry and good. I bought it from my niece Arndís at Meðalland.

Another twice-daily task is carrying water in thirty-litre containers on the quad bike to two places.

You also need to be careful choosing the ewes to put together in the stalls, with their newborn lambs. It doesn't work putting a timid ewe together with an aggressive one. The other day when Fanney was here, one of the ewes played a particularly mean trick. There were two of them in a stall with their newborn lambs. Then Fanney heard a loud crack: one ewe had butted the other's lamb so hard that blood poured from its nose – its skull had been cracked. That's unusual behaviour. The sheep normally just poke the lambs with their noses if the lambs annoy them, instead of butting them as hard as this one did.

We usually try to isolate the sheep we suspect of being in this kind of mood but we missed this one. It really upset us both and Fanney was still brooding over it even after she'd gone home. We felt as if we should have noticed it earlier. We immediately put the ewe with the injured lamb into a different stall, but the damage had been done and the lamb died a few hours later.

This and the many other things that can go wrong during lambing can really get to you. But then if you're lucky enough to possess something, you've also got to be capable of coping with losing it.

For four days in a row now, I've lost a sheep every day and had to bury it. It's remarkable that it's never a single sheep that dies; it's always more. And if one lamb goes, others tend to follow. This is such a large number of sheep that there are bound to be some casualties, but it always feels strange the way that they come in waves.

There's an ever-present worry of disease and contagion. The risk is greater when the sheep are crowded inside the sheep-houses. The danger increases the further into lambing you are, as the levels of heat and humidity rise in the sheep-houses. There's even a certain amount of risk when the sheep are in the paddocks outside the sheep-houses, as well as when they're in the fields. One morning several years ago, I lost ten lambs in a very short amount of time to colibacillosis. Birna and I reacted immediately and managed to stave off further losses by giving medication to all the other lambs.

The medications used in lambing cost a lot of money,

at least a hundred thousand krónur, all told. I dose my sheep with anthelmintics twice a year. It's absolutely necessary, to protect the sheep from eating for thousands of worms inside them. This medication also helps enhance fertility. And the lambs grow heavier, because they thrive better in a clean flock than a pest-ridden one. Icelandic sheep farmers generally use far fewer drugs than elsewhere, particularly penicillin.

In Iceland, veterinary control over penicillin and other antibiotics is very strict. In places where the sheep roam all year round in small, fenced pastures, as in Britain, anthelmintics are given monthly or bimonthly. Of course Iceland's colder climate helps, as well.

FÍFILL AND LAMBING

Fífill doesn't like it when he doesn't get to go with me when I'm doing things outside, so I've allowed him to hang around with me a lot during lambing. But he has to be constantly supervised around the lambs. He's still just a puppy, despite being so big, and I don't trust him completely yet. There's a risk that he could wound a lamb while playing with it, and in doing so, develop a taste for blood. It would take a huge amount of work to turn that round, and teach him better manners.

One additional problem during this lambing is that Fífill has lost so much weight that he's a bit weak, especially in his hind legs. I was afraid that something serious was up. Fanney came and took him to the veterinary clinic at Stuðlar near Selfoss, where X-rays were taken. It turns out that Fífill is suffering from over-exhaustion, and isn't getting enough nutrition. Dogs ideally need to sleep around sixteen hours a day, but he's been so excited to hang around with me that it has exhausted him. In addition, he's grown so rapidly that his muscles haven't had time to develop fully.

So it's a vicious circle: Fífill has little appetite due to

exhaustion. I've been trying to trick him into eating by pretending to give María's dog Ronja his food. But my friend Adda says that that isn't a very good method – that it could make Fífill overprotective of his food. She advised me to get him some frozen turkey necks and beef offal, which are supposed to be real treats for a dog.

It's as it always is with these pet projects: everything lands on my shoulders. Luckily, they're broad, and Fífill isn't strong enough to bust many ghosts in his state. So it looks like I'm just going to have to do it myself, then.

Fífill and Ronja are great friends. My old dog Frakkur, who's now eleven, is relieved when Ronja comes and takes the puppy's attention – and commotion – away from him. Frakkur has reached retirement age; he's stiff and fat and hobbles on one front leg when he's made to run. Otherwise, he's fit as a fiddle.

Old Frakkur gets really annoyed with Fífill. He scolds and growls, and Fífill, totally submissive, takes it all. I'm not looking forward to the inevitable day when Fífill finally snaps back. Right now, he completely respects Frakkur, so luckily there's no risk of conflict between them.

It's so much fun for Fífill when Adda brings his sister Rökkva. They play-fight and gambol around with each other.

My Fífill is spoiled, and expensive to maintain. I've just bought him a bigger crate, a mansion that's half the size of my bedroom.

THE ANXIETY BEAST

Depression is like being in a barrel that you can't see out of. I was so young when I first felt it that I didn't know what it was.

It was worst shortly after I took over the farm, but I haven't experienced it for years now. Back then I was often in pretty bad shape, but it never lasted long, maybe four or five days, with great highs in between. During the upswings, I worked and worked and worked.

Dad suffered from similar bouts of depression. Then he couldn't control his elation in between – he'd go a little bonkers and just have to play and play-fight with us girls. But the intensity of these mood swings lessened the older he became.

It was because of this that he didn't want me to take over the farm. He didn't want me to go through what he had. No one back then understood or acknowledged what depression was. People just described you as difficult.

Times have changed and Ljótarstaðir is no longer as isolated. The road is ploughed in the winter, and I have my Lux, a tractor and a snowmobile. And the Internet has made a big difference. So now my isolation is really my choice.

During periods of depression, everything goes black. When you're up, you know that the fits of depression end, but when you're in a trough, you can't see out. And your self-esteem is zero.

When I grew up and matured, I realized what this was. I knew that it would pass, knew what was happening and recognized the signs.

When depressed, I often stopped eating, just to be able to control something. Yet my appetite was still there, and it really isn't good for skinny scarecrows like me to stop eating.

I hit rock bottom one winter after a series of downswings from November until lambing. I must have been around twenty-five years old. This state can't be hidden while you're in it. Fanney and my other sisters knew about it, of course, and I could talk to them, but only as long as I wasn't actually in it. At such times, I couldn't talk about anything; I just struggled on through my work, surviving day to day.

I was too far away to seek help. To go into Selfoss or Reykjavik once a week isn't an option for a farmer deep inside Skaftafell District.

But I overcame it. It was a conscious decision. I decided to be a child of the sun. This is one of the many things that I've learned from Fanney, who always says that she's on the sunny side of life. And if you say it often enough, eventually you start believing what you tell yourself.

Everything also became easier once I managed to get a grip on the farm, after I came to own it and proved myself. When I gained full control, the farm operations started going better. I'd been fiercely determined not to turn thirty without owning anything. And now I owned the farm and had my own property, and that improved my self-esteem. Along the way I'd been fighting to prove myself, mainly to myself, and that had been very stressful.

Now I also began to come to better terms with the things that I couldn't handle, and to forgive myself for making mistakes. These kinds of things tend to come with age and greater maturity.

But I'll never forget how I felt the first times that I fell into the hole of depression. How low my self-esteem was – as it had always been, in fact. I spent ages, for example, convinced that I was the ugliest creature on earth.

When depression hits you full force, reason can't help you. Depression overwhelms all rationality. Luckily for me, however, my highs always lasted longer than my lows. I'd conquered my depression some time before my Depo-Provera disaster, and even though that floored me physically, it was nothing like as bad. Since then, I've realized better how lucky I am in life – to have good health and freedom, and to be a happy person who does well in life.

My experiences have made it easier for me to understand others; to understand people who are struggling with depression. With me, it was a kind of infantilism. I mainly overcame it through stubbornness, as with so many other things. The main thing is that I came to realize that everything passes, that all storms will eventually give way to sunshine, as my great-grand-father Bjarni from Vogur put it.

Now if I have a particularly difficult day during lambing and feel as if I'll never be able to get out of bed again, I know that a new day will come. When I get cold during pregnancy scanning, I know that I'll soon feel warm again. The fundamental thing is to remember that things will be okay. That it's all just a state of mind. But being the anxious character that I am, I have a tendency to let myself get clogged with worry over forthcoming tasks, particularly collaborative efforts such as round-ups. Stage fright is much worse than the actual performance. Things are always fine once I get going.

I've had stage fright before many events, such as meetings where I could expect conflict, and worried over them. Beforehand, I couldn't focus on anything, trembled and lost my appetite. It could throw me completely off balance to have to stand in front of people and maintain my composure. But it's getting better with practice.

There's no point in whining when we have it so good, generally speaking. One should also have the humility to be thankful for being born in Iceland, free from the horrors of war and destitution. Thankful for the blessing of having full bellies.

25 MAY

I lost a yearling last night. It was my fault. I tried to help her deliver, instead of just calling the vet immediately.

María and I were dealing with her. We discovered a long-dead foetus lying backwards in her uterus. This lamb was terribly large, and had already started to decay. I tried to straighten it out, but in so doing, tore the sheep's uterus. If I'd just quit right away and called the vet, the outcome would have been different. He could have done a C-section and she would have lived.

When I finally called him, he said that there was nothing he could do to save the sheep.

During dinner, nobody spoke. But then I decided to put the yearling out of her misery, and allowed myself a shot of Baileys before bed to numb my guilty conscience.

My first thought on waking the next morning was how badly I'd done. When you know you're the only one to blame, it's a hard thing to bear. And I'd thought I could get through to the end of lambing without mishap. There are now just twelve sheep waiting to give birth.

THE LAMB VAFNINGUR (WRAPPED)

In early summer, after lambing, it sometimes happens that lambs go astray from their mothers and roam around aimlessly. Or they might slip through a fence. Then they're motherless, and will end up stunted and ugly – if they survive. Of course, all sorts of things can lead to their deaths.

Lambs, however, have a tremendous will to live. Once I found myself with a two-day-old lamb with a broken thigh. The mother was a stressed yearling who'd either trampled the lamb or butted it badly. I'm quite good at putting splints on lambs with broken legs, but in this case, I couldn't do so because the fracture was so high up. I stabilized the leg and wrapped it with a compression bandage. The lamb was so small that the bandage covered most of it – so I gave it the name Vafningur (Wrapped).

The lamb, of course, was in terrible pain. Then I remembered the painkillers prescribed for my cat after she was neutered, and gave one to the lamb. It fell asleep so fast that I thought I'd finished it off for sure, so I went and poked it every now and then to check if it was alive. But it was just so tired that it slept like a rock as the pain decreased.

Lars the vet told me that the lamb would have to stay in the bandage for four weeks. I couldn't have put it with the other bottle lambs, because they would have trampled it. So I put it in a tub and gave it another little lamb to play with. And it grew bigger and fatter there within its stretchy wrap.

Meanwhile I tricked its mother into adopting a different lamb.

The lamb with the broken thigh healed fully and grew to become a fine, normal-sized sheep by that autumn. I'm quite proud of this cure of mine.

Now I have another lamb that can't stand up. It probably has a spine injury. It isn't sick, because it's drinking. We're milking the lamb's mother and bottle-feeding it. But once lambs become like this, they usually won't stand up again, so I have little hope that it will end up all right.

When I was growing up, sheep farmers didn't need so much help during lambing. The lambs were smaller, the ewes were on the move more and therefore in better shape, so it was easier for them to give birth. If something was wrong, you got someone to help, usually a neighbour. I wasn't trusted to help until I became older and tougher. You get better with experience, but you always end up messing something up.

I issue a stream of instructions to María and Sandra. I've asked them just to tell me to stop when they can't take any more. One of the things I've learned from my upbringing is to try to prevent mistakes before they happen. When I was young, no mistakes were made on the farm. Mistakes weren't an option – otherwise, you had a strip torn off you. My defence was mainly to try to escape the scoldings, but when I got bigger, I started just accepting them, to try to ward off the conflict between my parents. But because of all this, I hardly ever relaxed.

My dad had a hot temper, and was always impatient. I sometimes say that I was scolded to adulthood. It's undeniable, though, that having a constant knot in my stomach heightened the quality of my performance. These days, children's upbringing is completely different – they get endless compliments and pampering. I sometimes wonder if it doesn't produce complete wimps.

My friend Adda used to be an incredible help to me during lambing. She'd just finished school, knew little about lambing and said that she'd dreaded it. But she learned everything right away and was always so good-natured. She was happy having me as her tutor. She could also tell that I trusted her.

I was delighted when she told me that I'm good at delegating. That's apparently not a common thing on all farms, but it was the way we were brought up. On our farm, my dad was clever about allowing us sisters try out various tasks, and giving us all kinds of work.

Adda is the greatest animal lover that I've ever known. When we meet, we hardly talk about anything besides animals for hours, mainly our dogs, but also my sheep, living and dead. It's my experience that those who are animal lovers also love people – the two go hand in hand. Now Adda has her own farm and two kids. It's wonderful seeing her with her kids and to see her training Rökkva, ordering her to turn circles. Then her two-year-old boy joins in and makes the circles along with the dog, giggling and finding her terribly funny, which of course she is.

The maintenance of cleanliness and tidiness on the farm is vital. That applies particularly during lambing. Wounds on lambs can easily become infected, so the tagging tongs have to be clean, the iodine bottle clean. The forceps clean. And your hands must always be spotless during lambing. You've got to wash them constantly. As a consequence, my hands get ruined. My fingertips split open and bleed. The amnion around newborn lambs can be quite caustic. I haven't accustomed myself to wearing gloves doing this work as I'd have to be constantly changing them, and it would prove expensive. So I'm always washing my hands.

It's been only four years since I installed a hot water system and sink in the sheep-house, but it's been a revelation. Now I no longer have to bring everything back to the laundry room, including the bottles we use for milking. I installed the system myself. It wasn't a big deal. It's a small water heater that I unplug and disconnect from the sink once lambing is over.

Another job is keeping the sheep-houses tidy. Making sure the hay leavings don't pile up. Sweep, sweep and sweep. Luckily for us, María is very neat, and sweeps as we feel things should be swept. Cleanliness creates a good working environment in the sheep-houses, and it's also good for your head. Keeping things tidy helps you maintain your sanity.

Most importantly, lambing needs to be fun. It does no good seeing only the strife and fuss in all of it. When you aren't paralysed with exhaustion, it's easy to enjoy it. Now it's the three of us, so there won't be any moments of despair as there are when I'm alone and imagining everything falling completely apart.

Those lambs are so hilarious, especially when they're little. To see them trying to play when they're newly born, jumping for joy, even if they're in no shape for it and fall on their heads. There's such an incredible amount of playfulness in them; starting at about ten days old – they're like balls of energy. They often run around in groups inside the paddocks, back and forth, back and forth. When the sheep in the lamb house up here on the field are inside eating, there's so much room in the paddock that the lambs take the opportunity and zip all over and compete to see which one can get furthest up onto the lamb house roof.

It's a wonderful place, the lamb house at the top of the field next to the farm ravine. The old farmhouse ruins are right nearby – and the view across to Mýrdalsjökull. The houses are spacious, and the sheep are comfortable. After I feed the sheep, I enjoy watching the lambs play and act silly.

This spring has been so dry that the sheep are extremely comfortable. Total bliss. But everything has its advantages and disadvantages. The dry weather means that the grass is growing slowly, so the sheep will need to stay inside longer. Nothing is ever completely bad or completely good.

Some springs are like that; the wind blows from the north and north-west and not a drop falls from the sky. Normally, it's rather rainy here. Now the fields are in bad shape, with a great deal of winterkill from the ice last winter. In such droughts, the soil suffers and there's more erosion, with sand blowing over vegetated areas; so this kind of spring can be seen as bad for the land in some respects.

It's a huge milestone when I begin tidying up after lambing. When I start taking down the paddocks, and so forth. There's no use in leaving them up the whole year. They would just get ruined.

I can postpone putting down the lamb with the spine injury no longer. It can't stand up, and there's nothing else that can be done. But I really have to steel myself to take an animal's life. It's difficult, and puts me in a bad mood. I'm also fairly squeamish about it, which doesn't help. The first time I had to kill an animal, I puked my guts out.

I'm extremely careful about it. I make sure that the gun is in the right position and aim the barrel correctly. In the old days, Dad always did this. I had to force him to teach me how to use the gun when I was twenty. But I hate guns; I don't like killing things, it's just not in me. I couldn't imagine killing an animal with my bare hands, even a bird or a fish.

But it's awful seeing an animal in pain. If it's suffering, you have to ease its pain, or put it out of its misery. And of course a farmer has to be able to take care of this herself.

Dad was a cautious, tense man who carried the weight of the world on his shoulders, a weight that only increased after my sister's death. He was very careful with the gun and ammunition. And he didn't want us kids around when he had to put down an animal. I find that a good policy: keeping children away from such things. Dad had grown up in the days of less sophisticated technology, when guns didn't always fire properly and were much more dangerous. Early on, he had to learn to take matters into his own hands. When he was sixteen, he had to help his dad put down a horse. Grandpa's hands were so shaky that he couldn't hold the gun steady, so Dad took it from him and finished the job.

The worst thing is that not only do I have to put down this injured lamb, I also have to skin it, which I truly hate doing. But if I sew the skin around one of the extra lambs that's in need of a foster mother, one lamb from a set of three, the mother of the lamb I've just had to put down will then take on the new lamb in the old lamb's skin. Before I take the new lamb to her, I'll wash its head with soapy water in order to confuse her sense of smell. I'll then have to help the lamb start to suckle, because it's become so used to the bottle.

Then I'll have to remove the skin within twenty-four hours, or it will start to smell rotten.

Before I start to skin the lamb, I always wait some time to make sure that it's dead. Of course, this is just nervousness, because I know that it'll be dead for sure. But I get chills thinking of repeating an experience we had here once. María woke me up in the middle of the night to tell me that she simply couldn't bear to listen any more to the bleating of a sick lamb and that I had to do something. I'd only slept for two hours and my mind was in a haze. I shot the lamb and had started to skin it when it suddenly jerked. The lamb was dead and I knew that those were just nerve spasms, but it startled me terribly. My heart practically stopped. María said that my face turned chalky white.

Having to put down a lamb that has something wrong with it and will never recover, after holding it in my hands and trying to make things right, is one of the worst things that I have to do. The lamb has then become a kind of bottle lamb even though it's clear as day that it cannot get better. It's impossible not to start caring about a lamb that you've spent a lot of time with and that has started trusting you. In such cases, I have to work extra hard to make myself put the lamb down.

The success of lambing depends mainly on organization, so I spend most of April setting everything up. I have to order and buy the medications. Have all the equipment ready. Muck out the sheep-houses, move grates and blocks and all sorts of tools and things, set up the paddocks and get the sheep-houses and stalls into proper shape. I need huge amounts of space during lambing, because suddenly my flock grows by around eight hundred heads.

Lambing also involves a great deal of bookkeeping. This is something I detest, so I put it off as long as I can. My lambing team always carries notepads and pens, and we write down everything. Mum enters the information from the notepads into the sheep-flock register, which I then transfer to the computer.

I'm no real breeder. Ella, like all the best breeders, knows every sheep in her flock, whereas I know only a fraction of mine, and we've usually kept a similar number of sheep. I'm not interested enough in that aspect of it to pore over the books. I get terribly bored doing so, or even just thinking about it.

There are far more song lyrics and poems in my head than sheep pedigrees. A favourite of mine since my childhood is 'The Polar Bear' by Davíð Stefánsson. The first verse goes as follows:

Up north where the stars do coldly glow
o'er icy wastes in realms of snow,
once by chance men did ensnare
a fierce yet unwary polar bear.
Its defences slipped –
with ropes it was gripped,
and south to the king they it shipped.

*

Now there are only two ewes left to deliver. One's a yearling. She's driving me nuts. No foetus showed up on the ultrasound, but now she has a bulging lamb inside her. A ram must have got to her a week or ten days after I removed the rams from the yearlings; the ewes aren't supposed to give birth so late. It wouldn't surprise me if Gestur, the man who takes care of the feeding for me while I'm off doing pregnancy scanning, set this up as a practical joke, but the timing doesn't fit.

MONEY WORRIES

Money is my constant worry. Sometimes I can get so stressed about it that it makes me physically ill. That actually doesn't happen too often. But my finances are always pretty tight. I'm always worrying about the likelihood of something going wrong. What will I do if the tractor or the Lux breaks down? Or if one of the roofs blows off? It makes me more careful. I take good care of my equipment to make sure that it lasts a long time.

I'm no saver. Instead of building up reserves, I spend my money on travelling and seeing the world. And then I'll come up with other ways of spending whatever's left; for instance getting and maintaining my expensive ghostbuster, Fífill.

Once I tried to expand. It takes more than five hundred sheep for a farm to be self-sustaining, but my pastures are full. And it's quite a handful for a single worker to take care of so many sheep, whose number multiplies every spring.

When the couple at one of the farms at Snæbýli divorced, I made an offer for the farm. The Agricultural Association prepared a business plan according to the rules of the trade, and the bank agreed they would finance it. I would then have had twelve hundred sheep across two places, along with a beef-cattle operation. And I was going to use the farmhouse at Snæbýli as a guesthouse for tourists. Hiring staff for it, of course.

But then the wife decided to stick with farming, and they dropped the plan to sell the farm. Then when she changed her mind, it was sold within the family, and there's nothing wrong with that. It's good to have good neighbours, and not my dearest wish to be the only farmer in the valley. But it was a golden opportunity, and I would have been sorry if I hadn't tried to make it happen.

I try not to think about money too much; if I can keep things here afloat, that's enough for me. If I urgently need something, I don't search the Internet for days trying to find the cheapest deal but just buy whatever it is right away. I could probably save quite a bit of money if I were more of a patient shopper.

ÓLAFÍA

Ólafía Jakobsdóttir at Hörgsland in Síða is a pioneer in environmental conservation out here in the east. She was mayor for many years, and has been a passionate, if lonely, defender of nature for the longest time. She began speaking up for nature long before anyone else dared to call themselves conservationists or say out loud that they cared about protecting the environment.

Environmental conservation opens up new ways of thinking and new times and not everyone likes it. People can often be overwhelmed by how much things are changing. It's not as if all of those who support power plants are automatically polluters, or anti-conservationists: they can be people who respect the land and take good care of it, but who are unable to handle words such as conservation and environmentalist. They view them as symbols of a kind of aggressive cultural change. You could see this clearly in the debate about the expansion of the Vatnajökull National Park. The people who fought against it were worried that this expansion might mean everything would be closed and forbidden. And that then you couldn't let your sheep graze in the highlands and couldn't do round-ups there or sell fishing permits any more. This was not the case at all.

Here in Skaftá Municipality, there are energetic young farmers on many of the farms, and the population is growing. This is an excellent area for both agriculture and tourism and these mutually supportive sectors should obviously both be strengthened. We ought to be emphasizing leisure activities connected with agriculture here in this district, and of course promoting the produce of our farms – especially lamb meat.

Why are we waiting for someone to come and rescue us, only to turn round and destroy our land by building unnecessary power plants? We should be building up our lives and work without undermining everything we already have by allowing big industry to destroy our homes and our agricultural land.

We have everything we need to create the opportunities we want. I'm not suggesting that everyone should start changing bed sheets and chasing after sheep . . . these days, all you need is a good Internet connection and you can do almost anything. What we need is good fibre optic cables, not huge dams and vast reservoirs.

Ólafía Jakobsdóttir has been a great role model for environmental conservationists here in the east. We who follow in Ólafía's footsteps owe her a great debt of gratitude for the experience and knowledge that she has bequeathed to us.

HEIÐA AT A PUBLIC MEETING

Why has no progress been made in the development of new methods for generating electricity? Why do we always need to construct new reservoirs? The first computer filled an entire room, whereas today's computers are tiny. Reservoirs seem to be evolving in the opposite direction and becoming bigger and bigger. In the case of the Búland Power Plant, the plan is to flood ten square kilometres for the reservoir, and use another six square kilometres for quarries, roads, levees and all the other disruptions to the earth that come with the plant's construction. And then there are the transmission grids themselves: generators, substations, lines. I find it remarkable that more emphasis hasn't been put on advancing new electricity sources rather than relying on large numbers of people sniffing out new valleys to transform into mud puddles, and then into sandy wastelands.

I'm also allowed to feel this way. People can have opinions and feelings and express them! I know that this may sound an odd declaration coming from the mouth of someone from Skaftafell, but I'd like to remind you that I'm also a descendant of an emotional, dramatic poet from out west in the Dalir district, and I have strong emotional connections to my land. I believe that it's everyone's right to have feelings for the land. The use of it, and the way it's treated in general, shouldn't just apply to the oft-cited 'locals'. After all, although I don't live there, I certainly experienced deep emotional and mental lows over the oil refinery at Hvesta in Ketildalir in Arnarfjörður, and I didn't mince words expressing my views about the building of a container port in Finnafjörður.

THIS LAND OWNS YOU

The song 'Fylgd' ('Guidance') by the poet and farmer Guðmundur Böðvarsson holds a special place in the large lyric library in my head. I sang it loud and clear when I was little. All I wanted was to be the child in the song, with parents showing me the way and entrusting me with what was dearest to them. Whenever I thought through the words, I somehow felt them fully, with a kind of magical devotion, reverence and fortitude.

Often during the past few years, I've thought about this song and grinned to myself when it's played as the 'last song before the news' on Channel 1. Particularly these lines:

Grandpa, Grandma both lived here
as did Mum and Dad.
One short lifetime on this land
each of them they had –
through joy and sorrow, peace and strife.
This, though, you must not forget,
all throughout your life:
this land, your land –

it owns you.
If through dark doors
evil comes, with promises untrue,
there will be no need to choose –
this land you mustn't lose.

THE BÚLAND POWER PLANT
– A RESULT?

At the end of March 2016, the planned construction area of the Búland Power Plant was finally designated as protected. After all I'd been through, I couldn't trust this one hundred per cent, but my hopes were amplified tenfold that I would finally be left in peace to farm my land. I could think of nothing else the whole day when the news came. I'd been massively stressed in December and January, when the Suðurorka men were pressing hardest. I had no way of gauging the general mood across the community . . . I wasn't sure where my neighbours stood. Now the tension level has dropped, although I know we're still at risk. And Hólmsá is still in danger. The power plant planned there has only been put on hold.

But now everything feels different, even if the danger hasn't entirely passed. There's so much less tension in the district in general. I have a feeling that most people here are relieved.

The Suðurorka men's only hope would be if this decision were to be reversed in parliament, but it's unlikely that that will happen. One of the many things

I don't understand is why none of them came out east to see the big Skaftá River flood, which was a huge enough catastrophe to have swept all their plans off the table. Yet their plans remained as stupid and destructive as before, flying in the face of expert opinions.

I've spent years in a continual state of worry about new developments in the case: when those letters were coming from Suðurorka; when a meeting was scheduled, or whatever other bloody thing it might be. It's a very serious amount of added stress on us farmers when we're forced to deal with issues such as these. You're suddenly working either for or against them and find yourself getting caught up in the whole process in some way or another, being dragged here and there to read through stacks of files and reports. It's a huge added burden on people who have more than enough to do already. Naturally, this particularly applies to those in the Angling Association in my district who came to be involved in the Búland Power Plant matter under its auspices.

Environmental conservation is very different now than it was ten years ago. Far more groups are devoted to it, and far more people support it in general. My family and friends have backed me up, as have total strangers. Many farmers I've met during my pregnancy-scanning tours all over the country have declared: 'Stand your ground. This bullying is intolerable!' It's nonsense that everyone in the countryside supports power plants.

Of course, there are many others in my community who are opposed to the proposed plants at both

Búland and Hólmsá, even if they take no active part in the opposition. In my view, those of us who are prominent in the opposition are also fighting for these people.

My niece Arndís at Meðalland gave me a poster for Christmas, when the fight was at its peak. It says:

Stand up for what is right
even if you stand alone

I managed to remain standing because I had so much support and encouragement. Giving up was never an option. I was driven onwards. But I had to go to the meetings alone, of course, shaking with nervousness. And for several days ahead of those meetings, I would be consumed by anxiety. On the appointed days, I would literally end up shivering. Yet I had no choice but to put on some decent-looking clothes and just try to play it cool. One problem was my voice. Whenever I had to speak publicly, my jaw would stiffen, my voice would tremble and I couldn't talk clearly enough. As nobody listens to a person with a shaky voice, I had to learn how to get a handle on it for these forums.

After meetings and conferences and difficult phone calls, I often feel deflated because I've used up all my strength. I've been complimented and applauded, both of which help, of course, as does the knowledge that my contribution has mattered.

I have one tangible example of that. It was at a meeting with Suðurorka and the National Power Company, and the Industrial Affairs Committee of the Icelandic Parliament. A neighbour of mine had been invited to the meeting. He's opposed to the Búland Power Plant, but doesn't own land in the area that would be affected by it. As he's hardly a stakeholder, however, he didn't understand why he was invited. He let me know about this, and I rushed to the meeting, despite not being on the guest list myself.

One of the things that the Suðurorka men talked about was my ownership of five to ten per cent of the land that would be affected by the power plant. My response was to ask if they'd ever stood on a slope. If the land was flattened out, all the gorges, all the hills and so forth, then the whole picture would look completely different. As so often before, the Suðurorka men had no answer to that. They were clueless. It's fine, of course, if the enemy shoots himself. Then you don't have to waste lead on him.

I later heard that one of the major power-plant supporters on the Industrial Affairs Committee had changed his position after hearing me. It had made him aware of the special financial interests behind the project, and how much environmental damage the power plant could cause just by trying to harness the monster that is the Skaftá River, with the glacial floods that are so common to it.

But I found this meeting very painful, and was so upset when I came home that I drank half a bottle of white wine out on my deck just to try to calm myself down. I couldn't go to sleep; I had to try to relax instead of lying there in bed with heartburn.

This years-long fight has taken a noticeable toll on me. After one particularly difficult public meeting, a friend from the neighbouring community called to tell me that I had his and his wife's full support. They'd seen how strongly I'd felt about it, so strongly that there seemed to be little left of me! I couldn't have made it without phone calls like that. He also talked about how this had splintered our community, that people had lost their peace of mind. He worried that things here would never be properly mended. This thought has of course crossed my mind, but I was still surprised to hear it from him.

It's very clear that the methods employed by the energy industry have destroyed communities. The fight over the Þjórsárver area has been going on since 1950. The farmers in the Gnjúpverjar Municipality have been at the forefront in protecting this area, with which so few others were familiar. This vegetated highland area is one of the most splendid, valuable natural gems in all of Iceland.

In my opinion, it's scandalous that Þjórsárver is still under threat. Building a silicon-metal factory at Bakki in Húsavík is sheer foolishness. There were headlines in the papers announcing that the people of Húsavík were impatiently awaiting the building of the aluminium plant at Bakki – or something like that. But what about the people living there who don't want these factories? I can assure you that they certainly do exist.

I honestly didn't realize how big these projects can be until I saw their factory site. It's gigantic, probably twenty hectares: a massive industrial site slap bang in the middle of a natural paradise, not far from one of the most valuable salmon rivers in the country, Laxá in Aðaldalur. The visual impact is enormous, and it will also pollute the environment in many other ways.

THE FARM BETWEEN
VOLCANOES: PART 1

Katla the volcano is extremely active. As we're only about twenty-five kilometres away as the crow flies, the farm has often had to be abandoned in the past when it erupted. One upside of being on such high ground is that we aren't at risk from the floods that these eruptions cause, unlike the farms at Álftaver and Meðalland. But our buildings here do need to be well protected against the lightning that is a dramatic side effect of an eruption. Every child round here is brought up on the story of the maid in Skaftárdalur who died after being struck by lightning during an eruption in the nineteenth century.

The eruption in Eyjafjallajökull made me very anxious, because in the past Katla has often followed Eyjafjallajökull. When significant tremors were registered in Mýrdalsjökull Glacier in autumn 2010, I started obsessively reading the earthquake and volcanic activity reports day and night until the sheep were all back in the sheep-houses. If the volcano erupts in the summertime, you might well never find your sheep again.

Once Bárðarbunga began stirring, we quickly got ready to go and fetch the sheep from the highland pastures much sooner than planned. The round-up committee, along with everyone else, had long been aware that the sheep might have to be rounded up early. If there's a sub-glacial eruption, there will of course be ash fall, and Bárðarbunga isn't so far from the Skafártunga pastures.

In the north the farmers were simultaneously rounding up their sheep due to the risk of floods. But this time, as the eruption did not occur under Vatnajökull Glacier but at the Holuhraun lava field, there would be no subsequent glacial floods.

HEIÐA AT A POETRY MEET-UP

The gas from the Holuhraun eruption looked like a blue shadow on the hillsides of Skaftártunga, and it made such a striking, artistic picture that I couldn't stop thinking about it. This highlights another problem: sometimes my artistic side becomes obsessed with new ideas, and little gets done on the farm when it gains the upper hand.

Into her soul's window this poet does peer
and greets a bohemian shadowed with blue.
She wipes from her eye a hesitant tear –
then asks for a latte and green beret too.

THE FARM BETWEEN
VOLCANOES: PART 2

Bárðarbunga is fully loaded. It's not a question of whether it will erupt, but when. The same goes for Katla. The volcanoes beneath Vatnajökull have erupted numerous times throughout history, and Katla on average every fifty years. This is just the way this part of Iceland is.

Usually I don't think about this much. But the stories that I've heard! When my grandfather was a farmhand at Höfðabrekka in Mýrdalur, he witnessed, from high up on Höfðabrekka Heath, a glacial flood caused by Katla crashing down over Mýrdalssandur. He never forgot the horrific spectacle of the rushing rivers of dirty water and huge chunks of ice. And that was back in 1918, so Katla is certainly overdue for another eruption.

The Grímsvötn eruption was just a preview. It gave us a little taste of what could happen. We'd grown up on accounts of people being unable to see even their own outstretched hands in the ash fall. To which I and other people remarked dismissively: 'It'll be fine. We'll just turn on the lights; all vehicles today have lights.' We thought that we could treat it like ordinary darkness and drive through it, with our headlights and work lights blazing. But ash is totally different. When you turn on your tractor's work lights at night-time, you can still see for a long distance all around you. But in ash fall, these lights become glimmers that don't radiate outward. I didn't believe it until I experienced it for myself . . . stretching out my hand into the darkness, only to find it invisible.

It's surreal: no lights can be seen and no sounds can be heard. It made me admit defeat and start believing everything I'd heard. Sometimes it's good to see in black and white that modern technology can't save everything.

The eruption at Grímsvötn happened so abruptly that there was no time to be anxious. I found it much more bearable than being worried to death for days on end, uncertain of what might happen next. Luckily it happened towards the end of lambing, 21 May, when many of the sheep were still inside. I herded the rest of them back under cover, and then into the paddocks. It was brutal for the sheep, because there was so little space.

Mum and I were lucky that Arndís and her son were here, as we really needed their help. The ground was covered with ash; there was no grass to be had, and we had no idea how long the eruption would last. But there was no time for hysterics and handwringing. This was all about keeping things afloat with the sheep, making sure that those out in the paddocks had enough hay and a supply of unpolluted water.

It was extremely windy the day after the eruption. The ash was blown away, the ground was cleared and the sheep were able to graze again, so I let them out. Sheep can often be badly injured in ash storms; their eyes get full of ash and you have to rinse them out speedily to prevent them from going blind. It was much worse out east, particularly in the Fljót area, where some of the ewes and lambs were blinded.

For something I'd heard so much about, the ash fall proved completely unexpected. I couldn't see the light on the sheep-house from my doorstep, and it's only a short distance between them. Everything snuggled down and went to sleep. The geese down on the field thought it was night. The birds rested on the ground and went to sleep. I drove over a redshank with the quad bike and it only escaped death because it happened to be between the wheels. It shot up behind the quad, scared to death and utterly bewildered by the bike dashing over it. That has never happened before.

In one day, the Grímsvötn volcano belched the same amount of ash as came from Eyjafjallajökull in the whole of 2010. The ash gets into everything. It's a very fine dust that slips through every hole. There's still ash up on the rafters now.

We'd had masks and goggles ready since the Eyjafjallajökull eruption. Every day, teams from the Search and Rescue Service came to check if everything was okay and to offer their assistance if we needed it. Soon after the eruption ended, firemen came from town in a fire engine and hosed off the buildings with water.

Once it was over, I had to pound ash out of all the filters in all the vehicles and wash them thoroughly. I started with the Lux: washed, cleaned and vacuumed it. But when I turned on the heating system, ash blew out all over the interior, so I had to start afresh and clean it all over again. So with the next vehicle, I began by turning on the heating system. Ash kept blowing out of the system throughout the summer.

This eruption wasn't too serious because it lasted for such a short time and the strong winds helped to clear away most of the ash the next day. If it had gone on for weeks, the outcome would have been totally different. But when it was erupting at full strength the first day, there was no way of knowing how long it was going to last. The outcome, for me, was that this eruption left me much humbler about my neighbour Katla and the other forces of nature surrounding me.

HEIÐA AT A PUBLIC MEETING

My view is that I have no right to sell off Ljótarstaðir's land or water and thereby permanently damage this portion of the Earth that I've been entrusted with for my single lifetime. I wouldn't have wanted my mother or father or grandfather or grandmother to sell off the land in order to buy new lipstick or a Farmall tractor. We humans are mortal; the land outlives us. New people come and go, new sheep, new birds and so on, but the land, with its rivers and lakes, vegetation and resources, remains. It undergoes changes over the years, but it remains.

The history of human habitation at Ljótarstaðir is a long one, but it's far from continuous. Over the centuries, my neighbour, old Katla, has tried again and again to ruin Ljótarstaðir and other farms in Skaftártunga with ash and embers. But Katla's ash blew away and settled into the soil, and over time, vegetation always managed to regrow. Once the vegetation returned and the water ran clean once more, people returned with their animals – sometimes the same people that fled the eruption, sometimes new ones. But they settled in, put their livestock to pasture, grew grass and gathered hay. They lived and died, and then new people came along.

Ljótarstaðir didn't go anywhere, despite having been rendered uninhabitable for a time. The catastrophe passed and the land recovered. Power plants don't pass: they're irreversible and nothing can recover from them.

Let's not try to outdo old Katla.

From Byron, Austen and Darwin
to some of the most acclaimed and original
contemporary writing, John Murray takes pride in
bringing you powerful, prizewinning, absorbing
and provocative books that will entertain you
today and become the classics of tomorrow.

We put a lot of time and passion into what we
publish and how we publish it, and we'd like to
hear what you think.

Be part of John Murray – share your views with us at:

www.johnmurray.co.uk

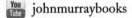 johnmurraybooks

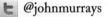 @johnmurrays

 johnmurraybooks